W9-BIB-916

Ashley J Bulliant

I'm Just Moving Clouds Today –
Tomorrow I'll Try Mountains.©

Books by Ashleigh Brilliant

(All Published by Woodbridge Press)

Books of Brilliant Thoughts®:

1. I May Not Be Totally Perfect, but Parts of Me are Excellent© (1979).

2. I Have Abandoned My Search for Truth, and Am Now Looking for a Good Fantasy© (1980).

3. Appreciate Me Now, and Avoid the Rush© (1981).

4. I Feel Much Better, Now That I've Given Up Hope© (1984).

5. All I Want Is a Warm Bed and a Kind Word, and Unlimited Power© (1985).

6. I Try To Take One Day at a Time, but Sometimes Several Days Attack Me at Once© (1987).

7. We've Been Through So Much Together, and Most of It Was Your Fault© (1990).

8. I Want To Reach Your Mind—Where Is It Currently Located?© (1994).

9. I'm Just Moving Clouds Today—Tomorrow I'll Try Mountains© (1998).

Other Books:

The Great Car Craze: How Southern California Collided with the Automobile in the 1920's (1989).

Be a Good Neighbor, and Leave Me Alone:© Essays and Other Wry and Riotous Writings (1992).

I'm Just Moving Clouds Today – Tomorrow I'll Try Mountains.©

And Other More or Less Blissfully Brilliant Thoughts.®

By *Ashleigh Brilliant*

Creator of Pot-Shots® and Author of
*I May Not Be Totally Perfect,
But Parts Of Me Are Excellent.*©

Woodbridge Press • *Santa Barbara*

WWW.ASHLEIGHBRILLIANT.COM

Published by

Woodbridge Press Publishing Company
Post Office Box 209
Santa Barbara, California 93102

Copyright © 1999 by Ashleigh Brilliant.

All rights reserved.

World rights reserved.

This book or any part thereof may not be reproduced in any form whatsoever without the prior written permission of Woodbridge Press Publishing Company, except in the case of brief passages embodied in reviews or articles pertaining to this book. Brilliant Thoughts® ("Pot-Shots"®) are each separately copyrighted. Up to but no more than five may be reproduced or quoted in a review of this book, provided the correct copyright acknowledgment is also included. Inquiries concerning all other uses of Brilliant Thoughts® ("Pot-Shots"®) should be directed to Ashleigh Brilliant, 117 West Valerio Street, Santa Barbara, California 93101, U.S.A.

Distributed simultaneously in the United States and Canada.

Printed in the United States of America.

Library of Congress Cataloging-in-Publication Data.

Brilliant, Ashleigh, 1933-
     I'm just moving clouds today—tomorrow I'll try mountains. : and other more or less blissfully Brilliant Thoughts® / by Ashleigh Brilliant.
          p.   cm.
     Includes bibliographical references.
     ISBN 0-88007-221-0   (pbk. :   alk. paper)
     1. Epigrams, American. I. Title
PN6281 . B675   1998
98-37805
818' .5402—dc21
CIP.

POT SHOTS® and BRILLIANT THOUGHTS®
are Registered Trade Marks.

Cover art: Janice Blair, Santa Barbara, California.
Reprint Credits: Globe Communications Corp., Boca Raton, Florida, p. 14; Pentland USA Design Group, Nashville, Tennessee, p. 18; the *Santa Barbara News-Press,* Santa Barbara, California, p. 20.

Dedication

To three wonderful friends
who, for strange reasons of their own,
have always had Faith in me:

My Wife, Dorothy
Our Helper, Sue McMillan
My Publisher, Howard Weeks

Acknowledgements

Special thanks to:

Robert Bernstein, Ian (Gene) Shadford, and (in fond memory) Greg Berman, for invaluable computer help.

Jack Goldenberg, for dreaming up the Ellesse deal.

Cynthia Hall Domine, for her licensing energy and savvy.

Glenn Carrico, for faithful years of Pot-Shots distribution.

Martin Needler, for touching me with his magic wand of academic respectability.

Lisa Kelly, for heroic service in the cause of B.L.A.S.T.

Herbert Hobler, for Brilliant Bagels.

And for no less deeply appreciated friendship, patronage, and help of many kinds:

Ron Kaufman, Gordon Hutchison, David and Marcia Karpeles, Mark Baldwin, Mike Hayward, Jim & Ellie Chastain, Sol Morrison, Randy Quinn, Lily Rossi, Richard Falcone, Rosie Nieper, Norman Cohan, Beverly Shapiro, Yorkman Lowe, Myra Orta, Harry Kislevitz, Gerald Werner, Pat McNamara, Ron Laurie, Hugh Mandesson, Brandy Brandon, Noel & Barbara Fleming, Caroline Weeks, Dorothy Weeks, Robin Holland, Bruce Gilberd, Pip Oatham, Linda Thornton, Mike Leibowitz, Neville & Glenda Auton, Warwick King, John Palminteri, Walt Hopmans, Gale Stoddard, Barney Brantingham, Steven Gilbar, Jack O'Connell, Ruth Dayes, Donald Sexton, Max Bromwell, Paul Lenze, Edward Yates, and Jan Knippers Black,

(hoping, of course, that each of them will buy several copies of this book.)

Contents

Introduction

Chapters

© ASHLEIGH BRILLIANT 1969.

POT-SHOTS NO. 118.

I'M JUST MOVING CLOUDS TODAY —

TOMORROW I'LL TRY MOUNTAINS.

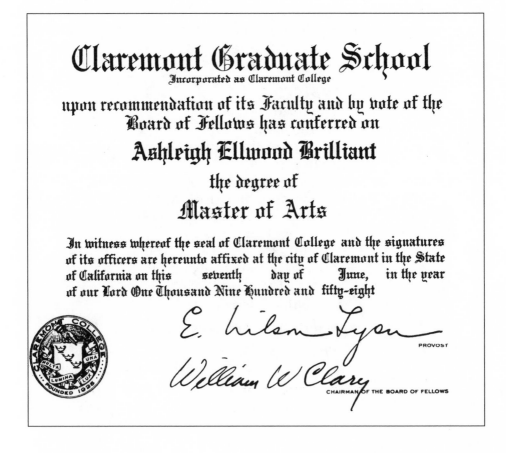

Claremont Graduate School
Incorporated as Claremont College

upon recommendation of its Faculty and by vote of the Board of Fellows has conferred on

Ashleigh Ellwood Brilliant

the degree of

Master of Arts

In witness whereof the seal of Claremont College and the signatures of its officers are hereunto affixed at the city of Claremont in the State of California on this seventh day of June, in the year of our Lord One Thousand Nine Hundred and fifty-eight

E. Wilson Lyon

PROVOST

William W Clary

CHAIRMAN OF THE BOARD OF FELLOWS

Introduction

Let's Do Launch

What is all this? What are we doing here? Presumably, I have something. Presumably, you want something. Won't it be wonderful if what I have turns out to be exactly what you want!

You are now entering my ninth book of illustrated epigrams, called Pot-Shots®, or Brilliant Thoughts®, which I originally began publishing as postcards in 1967. (Yes, Ashleigh Brilliant is my real name, and I am licensed to practice in the Arts—see documentary proof of both claims, opposite.) Just in case you haven't been here in my mind before, let me briefly go over the ground rules:

> Brilliant Thoughts are never longer than 17 words. They must be as different as possible from each other, and easily translatable into other languages. The words must be capable of standing alone, without any illustration. You are encouraged to think of them as one-line poems which may, without embarrassment, be shared aloud with consenting individuals or groups. Each Thought is separately copyrighted, and, when necessary, the copyrights are vigorously defended. All Pot-Shots are kept permanently available in postcard form through a very efficient catalogue and mail order service. (For details, see p. 167.)

I made all those rules myself, because I wanted to create my own ticket to Fame, Fortune, Freedom, Friends, and Fun. Fame was particularly important to me, but not just any old fame. I wanted to be recognized by the world's most eminent authorities. Unfortunately, there are not many world authorities on illustrated epigrams. In fact, by now I myself may be the most eminent one. Such are the rewards (or penalties) of being a pioneer. I've done a little better in the "Freedom, Friends, and Fun" categories. But Fortune—even on the scale of that enjoyed by my doctor, lawyer, or plumber—has so far been very elusive. Nevertheless, all this thinking has unquestionably made me older and wiser—or at least definitely older.

Theme Spirit

As with several previous books in this series, my Publisher felt that this one ought to have a theme— and, in view of the current popularity of angels and other divine phenomena, he proposed (bless him) that I turn my thoughts heavenward. I have always been intrigued by the uplifting idea that Faith can move mountains.[1] In 1969, that notion inspired me to write Pot-Shot #118, which has since then been consistently popular as a postcard, and which now put forward the winning claim to be the title of this volume. (Among the runners-up were: #1523, *I Want Eternal Life or Something Just as Good*, and #862, *There Really Is a God, but the Government Is Hushing it Up*.) Accordingly, FAITH is the duly ordained and officially sanctioned theme of these proceedings. But don't worry—you can (if you so choose) utterly ignore it, with no peril (that I know of) to your immortal soul.

Doting on Quoting

As a professional Epigrammatist, I naturally aspire to be legitimately, and if possible profitably, quoted, as widely as possible, by the most respectable people, for the best possible purposes. In previous volumes of this series I have, with, I hope, permissible pride (not unmixed with a little devilish de-

[1]In its New Testament form: "If ye have faith as small as a mustard seed, ye shall say unto this mountain, remove hence to yonder place; and it shall remove; and nothing shall be impossible unto you."—Mathew 17:20. In Islamic legend, the idea is turned around: Mohammed is asked to prove his own power by making Mount Safa come to him. Instead, the Prophet goes to the mountain, thereby proving his Faith in submission to God.

light) recorded some of the remarkable stages in my progress towards a still eagerly awaited Nobel Prize in Literature. Lately the pace of this advance seems to have accelerated. One indication is that my Thoughts, properly accompanied by my name, have at last begun to find their way into genuine, reputable works of reference. Three of the most notable such appearances are in current editions of (1) *The Penguin Dictionary of Twentieth-Century Quotations* (2) *The Harper Book of Quotations* (which in its Preface specifically mentions me, and recommends other writers of epigrams to follow my example and copyright their material), and (3) Louis A. Berman's *Proverb Wit and Wisdom* (which quotes no fewer than sixty-seven of my lines).[1]

These usages were all of course made with my permission, as have been a number of others, equally portentous in different ways, and covering a broad spectrum of Knowledge and—yes—Faith. In the latter category, I am, for example, sprinkled liberally throughout many of the works of Barbara Johnson, the celebrated "Queen of Encouragement," who has in recent years been a fixture on lists of best-sellers in Christian bookstores. The title of one of her books actually came from my Pot-Shot # 2313, *I'm So Glad You Told Me What I Didn't Want To Hear.*

Even more satisfying (since I myself am Jewish by background) was my recent first-ever appearance (in the form of 25 Pot-Shots) in a book of decidedly Judaic orientation, Joel Ziff's *Mirrors in Time: A Psycho-Spiritual Journey through the Jewish Year* (Jason Aronson Inc., 1996). And, in a related area, as many as forty-one Pot-Shots illuminate the pages of clinical psychologist Abe Arkoff's college-level textbook of self-discovery, *The Illuminated Life* (Allyn and Bacon, 1995).

[1]See me also in two collections by Bruce Lansky, published by Meadowbrook Press: *For Better and for Worse: The Best Quotes About Marriage* (1995), and *Age Happens: The Best Quotes About Growing Older* (1996).

In the realms of Knowledge, you will find me illustrating disciplines as diverse as Politics[1] and Sociology,[2] Management,[3] Medicine[4] and Psychology.[5] An Australian high school textbook uses Pot-Shots to stimulate students in their interpretation of an assigned novel.[6] And an American high school yearbook actually characterizes every member of the school faculty and staff with a different Pot-Shot. (The Assistant Principal, for example, is branded with #904: *Today I Hate You, but Try Me Again Tomorrow.*)[7]

Perhaps most gratifying of all to me personally, because of my deep interest in Conflict Resolution, is a book on that subject for use by elementary school teachers, which has on its cover both my title *Don't Shoot! We May Both Be on the Same Side* (Pot-Shot #680) and my illustration, of two people confronting each other from "opposite sides" of a Möbius strip.[8]

Press-tige

The mass media have also become at least a little more aware of my existence. *People* magazine and the *Wall Street Journal* had already discovered me (see Book 8)—but it was not until my debut in a notorious supermarket tabloid called the *Sun* that I felt I had really hit the Big Time (July 29, 1997—see illustration, p. 14). This paper's masthead disclaimer states that its stories "seek to entertain," and suggests that "the reader should suspend belief for the

[1] Martin C. Needler. *Identity, Interest, and Ideology: An Introduction to Politics.* Praeger, 1996.

[2] *Sociology: Australian Connections.* Allen & Unwin, 1997.

[3] Ron Garland. *Working and Managing in a New Age.* Humanics Ltd., 1989.

[4] David Wiesenberg. *Conquer Depression Now.* Mountain Meadow Press, 1996.

[5] William D.G. Murray. *Give Yourself the Unfair Advantage.* Type & Temperament Inc., 1995.

[6] Greg King and Mark Carey. *Into Fiction* 2. Rigby Heinemann, 1993.

[7] *El Potrillo*, Vol.22. Silver High School, Silver City NM, 1992.

[8] Kathy Beckwith. *Don't Shoot! ... A Curriculum Guide for Working Together and Resolving Conflicts.* Minneapolis: Educational Media Corp., 1998.

sake of enjoyment." I was therefore almost disappointed when the article about me (in an edition which also included RUSSIANS CLONING NEW BREED OF SUPER-SOLDIERS and ANGEL LEADS PILOT TO LOST GIRLS) turned out to be impeccably accurate.

Ironically, it was a much more mainstream newspaper, the Portland *Oregonian*, which dug up a truly sensational episode from my past, one which had erupted some three decades earlier, but which had (I thought) been virtually forgotten. And they featured it in an obituary! According to the *Oregonian* (October 2, 1994), Don P. Pence, a well-known educator, had died of a stroke at the age of 84. He had been president of Central Oregon Community College in the small town of Bend, but resigned in 1967,

> ... after dissident faculty members censured him for allegedly making decisions that were, in the words of Clay Shepard, then-president of the faculty forum, "arbitrary, tardy, and political." Among those decisions were Mr. Pence's firing of Ashleigh Brilliant for playing a tape recording of "Howl," a poem by Allen Ginsberg, which contained four-letter words Mr. Pence considered offensive. The college, Shepard said at the time, had "outgrown the president's ability to manage it."

Surprisingly (at least to me), the writer of this report apparently saw no need to identify me further in any way. I have rarely been back to Oregon since my first full-time college teaching job ended so dramatically there in 1965, and I never had any further contact with Mr. Pence. To be thus highlighted in his obituary was a unique distinction, and made me feel that I must indeed have had some lasting impact on the State of Oregon, if not yet on the whole nation.

Media Rare

But the whole nation is catching up, at least if you count appearances on nationwide TV, of which I have recently made my first two, though neither was such as to cause any established TV luminary to shake in his shoes. In one, I am seen for about twelve

Courtesy of Globe Communications Corp., Boca Raton, Florida

True Fame. See Press-tige, *pp. 12, 13.*

seconds (sitting in a model-T Ford), and heard for several minutes, speaking as an expert on how the automobile affected Southern California in the 1920's (the subject of my book *The Great Car Craze*).[1] In the other, a ten-minute CBS segment about my extraordinary career as professional thinker, I am shown working, jogging, performing, and reflecting, amid my daily home surroundings.[2]

Title Waive

Protecting my copyright continues to be a major tribulation of this peculiar profession. Powerful forces of infringement still rear their ugly heads from time to time, which I must confront, armed only with righteousness (and some expensive lawyers). In 1996, David Brinkley, who had for several decades been one of America's best-known television news personalities, published a book with a title virtually identical to Pot-Shot #461, *Everybody Is Entitled To My Opinion*, which I had written and copyrighted in 1974.[3] He actually admitted in the book that he himself did not originate the title, but said he had paid a $1000 reward to the family friend by whom it had been "thought up."

Upon learning of this, I immediately wrote to Mr. Brinkley suggesting, as respectfully as I could, that, as the original author and copyright holder, I was at least entitled to the same amount he had paid someone else for the title. I pointed out the possibility that his friend had somewhere come across my widely-circulated expression, and had, perhaps unconsciously, been quoting it. Through his publisher's lawyers, we reached an agreement (dated January 8, 1997) whereby I permitted him to use the title, and received in return $1000, and a promise that I would

[1]In Part 2 of the Resolution Productions documentary, "California and the Dream Seekers," first broadcast on the Arts & Entertainment Network, January 19, 1998.

[2]Produced by CBS News. First broadcast on the program "Off Tenth" on the "Eye On People" Network, April 7, 1997.

[3]David Brinkley. *Everyone Is Entitled to My Opinion.* Knopf, 1996. Paperback edition: Ballantine Books, 1997.

be credited in any future printings of the book. That seemed to me a fair and satisfactory settlement. I was therefore very surprised to read a report in the *Wall Street Journal* on January 27, 1997, that Mr. Brinkley had described the whole transaction as a "shakedown."

Coming from a man who must know the importance of choosing words carefully, that was an astonishing allegation.[1] Every dictionary I consulted defined "shakedown" as a criminal act, such as blackmail or extortion. This placed me in a difficult situation. If you doubt me, ask yourself when was the last time you were falsely accused, by a widely respected news authority, of engaging in a criminal activity? I had to do something, or my entire career, which is based on claiming these epigrams as my legitimate intellectual property, might be in jeopardy. Once again I wrote to this media icon, pointing out that such an unfair statement, coming from such an authoritative source, was very harmful, and politely asking him for an apology. I had no idea if I would get one, or if I would be left with the unpleasant option of suing a man who was still one of the country's most highly regarded public figures for libel.

David Brinkley's personal reply happened to arrive at my house at the very time I was being filmed there by the CBS News crew (March 10, 1997). This gave me the magnificent opportunity to open and read it on camera—an unusually dramatic moment (in my normally placid existence), which actually became part of the broadcast segment. To my great relief, the letter was indeed a sort of apology—not a very gracious one, but at least enough to make me feel, and thereupon announce to the nation, that honor had been satisfied. Very shortly thereafter, Mr.

[1]But slightly less astonishing, in view of a somewhat similar incident only two months earlier in which he had made some strangely inappropriate remarks about the President on national TV, and subsequently apologized for them.

ber 10, 1997, in East Windsor, New Jersey.[1] The extraordinary decor of this establishment included various Brilliant Thoughts emblazoned on its dining-tables, walls, and even the drinking-cups. Customers waiting for service were entertained with Pot-Shots flashed on a screen. There was no budget to bring me in person for the grand opening, but I am told that my portrait, a la Colonel Sanders, was also prominently displayed.

A Gleam of Academe

All such achievements count very little, however, in comparison with the academic recognition which I still so desperately crave, and which is still being widely withheld, perhaps because, (quite intentionally) what I am doing does not fall within any established category. But I did at last receive and, (with pathetic gratitude), accept, an invitation to speak about my work at one genuine University. The rarity of that paid appearance was at least a little redressed by the fact that the same institution (after taking a few years to recover) actually endured a return engagement (University of the Pacific, Stockton, California, Feb. 16, 1994, and July 31, 1997).

Blown Away

My biggest recent accomplishment, however, at least in terms of local acclaim, had nothing at all to do with Pot-Shots. It was my successful campaign against the ghastly gasoline-powered, noise-making, dirt-blowing devices called "leafblowers," which for many years had been permitted to pollute my home town. The Santa Barbara City Council, to its eternal discredit, had refused time after time, despite the example of many other cities, to take effective action against this plague.

In the absence of any truly competent leader for such a cause, I myself, though clearly a charisma

[1] "Mike's Brilliant Bagels," in the Windsor-Hights Shopping Center at Routes 130 and 571.

SANTA BARBARA
News-Press

The voice of Santa Barbara County since 1855   Thursday, November 6, 1997

MIKE ELIASON/NEWS-PRESS PHOTOS

Anti-blower activist Ashleigh Brilliant says the city has turned over a new leaf with the ban.

Blower foes eagerly await a broom town

By NORA K. WALLACE
NEWS-PRESS STAFF WRITER

Ashleigh Brilliant has the perfect epigram to describe how he achieved victory in his drive to ban gas-powered leaf blowers in Santa Barbara.

"If you want things to be quiet, you sometimes have to make more noise than anybody else," states Brilliant's Pot-Shots No. 1412.

There's also an apropos message in No. 4108: "How can noisy machines help clean the world, when noise itself is a form of filth."

Since the 1970s, Brilliant — the syndicated author of such pithy statements — has been a strident, aggressive, seemingly indefatigable champion in the effort to rid Santa Barbara of leaf blower noise and dust.

On Tuesday night, 54.5 percent of those voting passed a ballot measure to ban the use of gas-powered blowers. In the city, just 17,498 of the 58,515 registered voters — or just under 30 percent — cast ballots.

Starting Feb. 2, use of the blowers will be prohibited citywide. The measure does not include electric leaf

ELECTIONS '97

■ Final results from Santa Barbara County races. **A14**

Deciding not to wait for the ban to take effect, city parks officials already have abandoned their machines.

blowers or other gardening machines.

Although that's a three-month transition period, the city's Parks and Recreation Department stopped using the machines Wednesday.

"The way I look at it, the citizens said, 'We don't

DETAILS

Starting Feb. 2, it will be unlawful within the city limits to use or operate any portable machine powered with a gasoline engine, or gas powered generator, to blow leaves, dirt and other debris off sidewalks, driveways, lawns or other surfaces.

Electric blowers are still allowed, with certain restrictions:

● They are prohibited within 250 feet of a residential zone before 9 a.m. and after 5 p.m.

● They cannot be used at all on Sundays or national holidays.

● Electric blowers can be used at any hour in a commercial zone as long as they are not used within 250 feet of a residence.

Courtesy of the Santa Barbara News-Press

See Blown Away, *pp. 19-21.*

cripple, reluctantly assumed that role. I organized a group called B.L.A.S.T. (Ban Leafblowers And Save our Town), and we mounted an Initiative action to put the issue on the ballot (a democratic procedure not yet available in all countries, or even in all U.S. states). This project required securing thousands of signatures, and took months of grinding effort. There was, of course, opposition from entrenched interests— but we could feel success blowing in the wind. On November 4, 1997, by a substantial majority, the voters of our city imposed a total ban on those infernal instruments. As a result, I find I am enjoying not only a more livable community, but an enhanced image. Instead of (or at least in addition to) being a mere oddball, I am now something of a local hero. (See illustration, p.20.)

*** *** ***

Victories of this kind—and of many other kinds— are of course ultimately won in people's hearts and souls. But the topography of those regions is often beset with enormous barriers to clear thinking. If any such mountains are still obstructing your own view of the universe, I hope that what follows here may help move them. At least let us acknowledge that the attempt is being made in good Faith.

I. Self Addressed

Seeking Faith is like looking for a lost flashlight in the dark. You really need to have it in order to find it. But we must start somewhere—and if you can't believe in yourself, what can you believe in? Answer: just about anything else you choose (as will be abundantly demonstrated hereinafter). Nevertheless, the SELF has a compelling fascination. It's always there. It never abandons you, no matter how hopeless a mess you make of your life. Not only that, it understands—it sympathizes. In the face of this unshakable loyalty, the strange thing is how unappreciative we tend to be—so much so that there is now a whole industry devoted to teaching us how to "esteem" our Selves.

I personally have never had that problem. My own Self gets so much esteem that it tends to become arrogant. It has its own agenda, quite at variance from mine, and will sometimes go on strike altogether, until it gets the movie, the walk, or the chocolate it thinks it needs.

Still, I believe in it. I know that when the chips are down (not even counting the chocolate chips), my Self is on my side. And I'm confident that you, with any luck at all, are finding your own Self equally dependable. So let's begin our investigation of Faith with an intimate visit to this most faithful of entities, the one which, somewhat confusingly, you and I both call "me."

©ASHLEIGH BRILLIANT 1995.

POT-SHOTS
NO. 6907.

MY BIGGEST PROBLEM

IS THAT
I HAVE
NO ONE TO BLAME
BUT MYSELF.

Ashleigh Brilliant
SANTA BARBARA

©ASHLEIGH BRILLIANT 1993. SANTA BARBARA.

POT-SHOTS NO. 6572.

Ashleigh Brilliant

IT'S EASIER TO SEE OUT OF MY HEART

THAN IT IS
TO SEE IN.

Ashleigh Brilliant
SANTA BARBARA

POT-SHOTS NO. 5393.

I NEVER GO ANYWHERE

WITHOUT
MY
FAULTS.

©ASHLEIGH BRILLIANT 1991.

© ASHLEIGH BRILLIANT 1993 · SANTA BARBARA. POT-SHOTS NO. 6354.

MY HEAD NEVER LIES TO MY HEART ~

BUT MY HEART SOMETIMES TELLS LITTLE FIBS TO MY HEAD.

POT-SHOTS NO. 1632.

SOMETHING MUST BE WRONG SOMEWHERE

BUT WHY IS EVERYBODY LOOKING AT ME?

Ashleigh Brilliant   © ASHLEIGH BRILLIANT 1973.

POT-SHOTS NO. 6373.

IT'S AN UNEQUAL RELATIONSHIP:

the world doesn't need me nearly as much as I need the world.

© ASHLEIGH BRILLIANT 1993 SANTA BARBARA.

Self Addressed   25

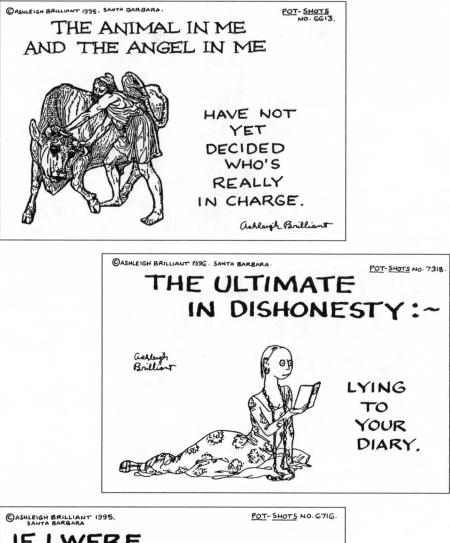

© ASHLEIGH BRILLIANT 1995. SANTA BARBARA.

POT-SHOTS NO. 6613.

THE ANIMAL IN ME
AND THE ANGEL IN ME

HAVE NOT
YET
DECIDED
WHO'S
REALLY
IN CHARGE.

Ashleigh Brilliant

© ASHLEIGH BRILLIANT 1996. SANTA BARBARA.

POT-SHOTS NO. 7318.

THE ULTIMATE
IN DISHONESTY :~

LYING
TO
YOUR
DIARY.

© ASHLEIGH BRILLIANT 1995.
SANTA BARBARA

POT-SHOTS NO. 6716.

IF I WERE
IN FULL CONTROL
OF MY LIFE,

I WOULD
GET
SOMEBODY
ELSE
TO LIVE IT.

Ashleigh Brilliant

© ASHLEIGH BRILLIANT 1995. SANTA BARBARA.   POT-SHOTS NO. 6744.

I MAY NEVER KNOW MY REAL VALUE,

Ashleigh Brilliant

UNTIL I'M KIDNAPPED, AND HELD FOR RANSOM.

© ASHLEIGH BRILLIANT 1995. SANTA BARBARA.   POT-SHOTS NO. 6778.

I HAVE TO BE CAREFUL WHEN TALKING TO MYSELF,

BECAUSE I'M VERY EASILY OFFENDED.

Ashleigh Brilliant

© ASHLEIGH BRILLIANT 1995. SANTA BARBARA.   POT-SHOTS NO. 6791.

IT'S HARD TO KEEP MY LIFE IN BALANCE,

Ashleigh Brilliant

when I don't really know where its center is.

©ASHLEIGH BRILLIANT 1995. SANTA BARBARA.

POT-SHOTS NO. 6797.

YES, BUT IT'S ONLY MY UNREALISTIC EXPECTATIONS

THAT ARE KEEPING ME ALIVE.

Ashleigh Brilliant

©ASHLEIGH BRILLIANT 1995. SANTA BARBARA

POT-SHOTS NO. 6836.

Ashleigh Brilliant

IT SEEMS THE WORLD WAS DESIGNED TO MAKE ME FEEL SMALL, AND MY PROBLEMS FEEL BIG.

©ASHLEIGH BRILLIANT 1995. SANTA BARBARA

POT-SHOTS NO. 6971.

MY ONLY REASON FOR STAYING ALIVE

IS THAT IT GETS ME A CERTAIN AMOUNT OF ATTENTION.

Ashleigh Brilliant

©ASHLEIGH BRILLIANT 1996. POT-SHOTS NO. 7409.

I DON'T WANT
TO BE
BETTER THAN
EVERYONE
ELSE ~

I JUST WANT
TO BE BETTER
THAN MYSELF.

Ashleigh Brilliant
SANTA BARBARA

©ASHLEIGH BRILLIANT 1998. POT-SHOTS NO. 7622.

OH HOW I WISH

I COULD
STOP WISHING!

Ashleigh Brilliant
SANTA BARBARA

©ASHLEIGH BRILLIANT 1998 POT-SHOTS NO. 7648.

INCLUDING MYSELF,
TWO PEOPLE
ARE ON
MY SIDE ~

(BUT I MAY HAVE
COUNTED
ONE OF THEM
TWICE).

Ashleigh Brilliant
SANTA BARBARA

©ASHLEIGH BRILLIANT 1998. SANTA BARBARA.

I WISH I COULD GO BACK TO BEING

WHAT I KNOW I NEVER REALLY WAS.

Ashleigh Brilliant

©ASHLEIGH BRILLIANT 1998. SANTA BARBARA

TO MOST OTHERS, I'M NOT VERY IMPORTANT,

and yet, to myself, I'm absolutely essential.

Ashleigh Brilliant

©ASHLEIGH BRILLIANT 1998. SANTA BARBARA.

THERE'S NO WAY OF DISGUISING THE FACT ~

MINE IS OBVIOUSLY A USED FACE.

Ashleigh Brilliant

© ASHLEIGH BRILLIANT 1998
SANTA BARBARA

POT-SHOTS
NO. 8065.

SOME
OF THE
PROMISES
I'VE MADE
TO MYSELF

WERE MADE
UNDER DURESS.

Ashleigh Brilliant

© ASHLEIGH BRILLIANT 1998. SANTA BARBARA.

POT-SHOTS NO. 8089.

Ashleigh Brilliant

THE LAW AGAINST
LONELINESS
HAS BEEN
REPEALED,

BUT
NOBODY
WANTS
TO CELEBRATE
WITH ME.

© ASHLEIGH BRILLIANT 1998. SANTA BARBARA.

POT-SHOTS NO. 7695.

Ashleigh Brilliant

LIFE
WILL GO ON
WITHOUT ME,

BUT
IT WON'T
SEEM
QUITE THE SAME.

Self Addressed 33

34

II. Life Sighs

Still looking for something to believe in? LIFE itself may be just the ticket for you. No sharp edges. (Everything somehow merges into everything else.) Safe for children and pets (in a manner of speaking). But enough mystery to build whole religions on. Believe in Life! Persuade yourself that what you seem to be experiencing really is happening—the agony, the ecstasy, the monotony.

Life is the name of that famous "same boat" we are all in (except that every now and then one of us disappears over the side). I myself came aboard in 1933, a year which (at this writing) will soon be not only in a past Century, but in a past Millennium. Nothing, it seems, can be done about this—except possibly to adopt some new calendar.

Whenever nothing can be done about something, people tend to say "That's life!" as if those words were some kind of explanation or consolation. Often they say it in French: "C'est la vie," perhaps in unconscious tribute to the thoughtful Frenchman who first popularized the whole game of believing in Life, with his sensational slogan, "I think, therefore I am." (Most of Descartes' other writings were considerably longer, so I don't consider him a serious rival as an epigrammatist.)

In my case, what the Life game comes down to is a card game. All of my Thoughts circulate openly on postcards, and pass freely through the mails, despite the possibility that some of them are intellectually explosive. To that extent, Life may not be quite so safe after all. Proceed into this chapter, therefore, with great caution—and if you think you want to continue being, be sure to continue thinking.

© ASHLEIGH BRILLIANT 1993. SANTA BARBARA.

POT-SHOTS NO. 6219.

I DIDN'T
ASK
TO BE
BORN ~

BUT THEN,
WHO DID?

Ashleigh Brilliant

© ASHLEIGH BRILLIANT 1993. SANTA BARBARA.

POT-SHOTS
NO. 6559.

Ashleigh
Brilliant

NO MATTER
HOW SHORT
LIFE
MAY SEEM,

it's surprising
how much trouble
there is time for.

© ASHLEIGH BRILLIANT 1993.

POT-SHOTS NO. 6512.

Ashleigh
Brilliant
SANTA
BARBARA

WHAT
I MOST
WANT
FROM LIFE

IS TO KNOW
WHAT LIFE
WANTS FROM ME.

© ASHLEIGH BRILLIANT 1993. SANTA BARBARA.   POT-SHOTS NO. 6227.

NO MATTER HOW MANY GOOD STEPS YOU TAKE, A SINGLE BAD ONE CAN END YOUR WHOLE JOURNEY.

© ASHLEIGH BRILLIANT 1996 SANTA BARBARA   POT-SHOTS NO. 7089.

IT ONLY HURTS WHEN I THINK OR FEEL.

Ashleigh Brilliant

© ASHLEIGH BRILLIANT 1996. SANTA BARBARA.   POT-SHOTS NO. 7200.

THERE'S NOTHING MUCH I REALLY NEED, EXCEPT A BETTER LIFE.

Ashleigh Brilliant

© ASHLEIGH BRILLIANT 1985.   POT-SHOTS NO. 3608.

You can't order everything on the menu of life.

Ashleigh Brilliant

© ASHLEIGH BRILLIANT 1995.
SANTA BARBARA   POT-SHOTS NO. 6616.

I'VE BEEN GIVEN A SMALL ROLE IN A MYSTERY-DRAMA CALLED LIFE,

IN WHICH ALL THE CHARACTERS DIE.

Ashleigh Brilliant

© ASHLEIGH BRILLIANT 1995.   POT-SHOTS NO. 6630.

CAN IT BE THAT MY WHOLE LIFE IS A DETOUR,

Ashleigh Brilliant
SANTA BARBARA

AND I WAS REALLY GOING SOMEWHERE ELSE?

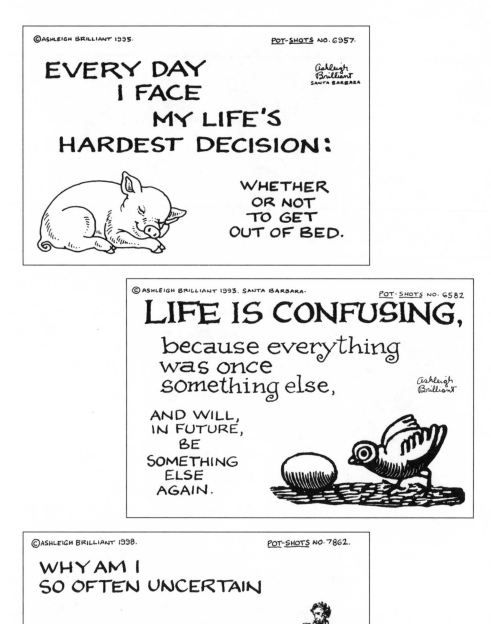

© ASHLEIGH BRILLIANT 1995.   POT-SHOTS NO. 6957.

**EVERY DAY
I FACE
MY LIFE'S
HARDEST DECISION:**

Ashleigh Brilliant
SANTA BARBARA

WHETHER
OR NOT
TO GET
OUT OF BED.

© ASHLEIGH BRILLIANT 1993. SANTA BARBARA.   POT-SHOTS NO. 6582

LIFE IS CONFUSING,
because everything
was once
something else,

Ashleigh
Brilliant

AND WILL,
IN FUTURE,
BE
SOMETHING
ELSE
AGAIN.

© ASHLEIGH BRILLIANT 1998.   POT-SHOTS NO. 7862.

WHY AM I
SO OFTEN UNCERTAIN

WHAT TO
HOLD ON TO

AND WHAT TO
LET GO OF?

Ashleigh
Brilliant
SANTA BARBARA

© ASHLEIGH BRILLIANT 1993, SANTA BARBARA.

THINGS ARE SOMETIMES BETTER LEFT AS THEY ARE,

BUT YOU CAN'T BE SURE UNTIL YOU CHANGE THEM.

© ASHLEIGH BRILLIANT 1995.

LIFE IS SHORT:

HAVE ANOTHER PIECE OF CHOCOLATE.

© ASHLEIGH BRILLIANT 1998.

HOW CAN LIFE BE SO SAD

AND SO RIDICULOUS

AT THE SAME TIME?

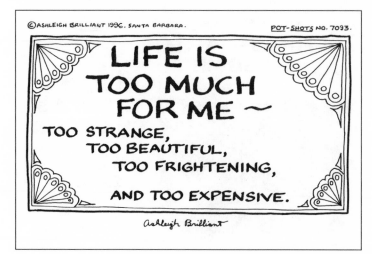

©ASHLEIGH BRILLIANT 1996. SANTA BARBARA. POT-SHOTS NO. 7093.

LIFE IS TOO MUCH FOR ME ~
TOO STRANGE,
TOO BEAUTIFUL,
TOO FRIGHTENING,
AND TOO EXPENSIVE.

Ashleigh Brilliant

©ASHLEIGH BRILLIANT 1998. SANTA BARBARA POT-SHOTS NO. 7789.

LIFE MAY BE TRYING TO TELL ME SOMETHING,
BUT I'M AFRAID IT'S NOT A FRIENDLY MESSAGE.

Ashleigh Brilliant

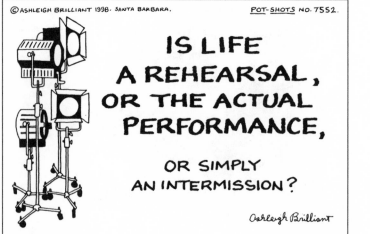

©ASHLEIGH BRILLIANT 1998. SANTA BARBARA. POT-SHOTS NO. 7552.

IS LIFE A REHEARSAL, OR THE ACTUAL PERFORMANCE,
OR SIMPLY AN INTERMISSION?

Ashleigh Brilliant

©ASHLEIGH BRILLIANT 1996.   POT-SHOTS NO. 7291.

LIFE IS WONDERFUL,

AND YET
THEY SAY THAT,
IF YOU DON'T HAVE IT,
YOU DON'T MISS IT.

Ashleigh Brilliant
SANTA BARBARA

©ASHLEIGH BRILLIANT 1993.   POT-SHOTS NO. 6540.

DO SOMETHING IMPORTANT WITH YOUR LIFE:

ENJOY IT!

Ashleigh Brilliant
SANTA BARBARA

©ASHLEIGH BRILLIANT 1998 · SANTA BARBARA.   POT-SHOTS NO. 7804

I HAVEN'T TIME TO MAKE ANY NEW MISTAKES TODAY ~

I'M TOO BUSY
CORRECTING YESTERDAY'S
MISTAKES.

Ashleigh Brilliant

© ASHLEIGH BRILLIANT 1998.

POT-SHOTS NO. 8002.

LIFE MIGHT BE A MORE ENJOYABLE GAME,

Ashleigh Brilliant
SANTA BARBARA

IF WE DIDN'T HAVE TO PLAY IT ALL THE TIME.

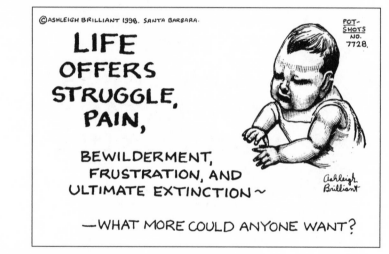

© ASHLEIGH BRILLIANT 1998. SANTA BARBARA.

POT-SHOTS NO. 7728.

LIFE OFFERS STRUGGLE, PAIN,

BEWILDERMENT, FRUSTRATION, AND ULTIMATE EXTINCTION ~

Ashleigh Brilliant

—WHAT MORE COULD ANYONE WANT?

© ASHLEIGH BRILLIANT 1996.

POT-SHOTS NO. 7065.

MY LIFE IS A STORY OF TRIUMPH ~

IT'S ABOUT ALL THE THINGS THAT HAVE TRIUMPHED OVER ME.

Ashleigh Brilliant
SANTA BARBARA

44

© ASHLEIGH BRILLIANT 1983.

POT-SHOTS NO. 2857.

WHY IS IT SO MUCH EASIER
TO PREDICT
THE MOVEMENTS
OF PLANETS
THAN
THE
BEHAVIOR
OF PEOPLE?

Ashleigh Brilliant

III. All the Humanity

What is the truth about PEOPLE? Can we really believe in them, or would we be better off believing in something with a track record less dappled with disappointment and frustration? Faith in Humanity used to be all the rage. Strange as it seems, for hundreds of years the armies of various nations enthusiastically sang about human brotherhood as they marched off to kill each other. The real enemy, it seemed, was not other people, but simply their wrong ideas. Human beings were infinitely perfectible, if only they would do things, see things, believe things, our way.

Unfortunately even today, after so much whipping of each other into shape, it is still easier to move mountains than it is to change some desperately misguided minds. And certain people, just as human as you or I, persist in doing things which give Humanity a bad name. Some grab the headlines with multiple murders and other horrendous acts. But just as uncivilized in their own way are those unsung evildoers who drop litter, fail to flush toilets, and unthinkingly torment their fellow humans with noise.

In the face of such embarrassments, it seems obvious why the worship of Humanity no longer seems to have much chance (except perhaps among dogs) of achieving the status of a major religion. As a subject for study, however, this very large demographic group has many advantages, specimens being widely available for observation in all kinds of habitats. As a card-carrying member, I can readily attest to some of our more peculiar characteristics—especially since the cards I carry, as here displayed, are those I myself have issued and validated.

© ASHLEIGH BRILLIANT 1996
SANTA BARBARA

POT-SHOTS NO. 7058.

THINK
TOO LITTLE,
AND PEOPLE WILL
CALL YOU STUPID~

THINK
TOO MUCH,
AND THEY'LL
CALL YOU CRAZY.

Ashleigh Brilliant

© ASHLEIGH BRILLIANT 1998. SANTA BARBARA.

POT-SHOTS NO. 8027.

MY APPEAL
FOR HELP

WAS MET
BY A GREAT
OUTPOURING
OF
APATHY.

Ashleigh Brilliant

© ASHLEIGH BRILLIANT 1996. SANTA BARBARA.

POT-SHOTS NO. 7336.

SOME
PEOPLE
WILL DO
ANYTHING
TO GET
ATTENTION,

EXCEPT
DESERVE IT.

Ashleigh Brilliant

© ASHLEIGH BRILLIANT 1993. SANTA BARBARA.   POT-SHOTS NO. 6168.

NO GROUP IS COMPLETE

WITHOUT
AT LEAST ONE MEMBER
WHOM EVERYBODY ELSE
REGRETS HAVING IN THE GROUP.

Ashleigh Brilliant

© ASHLEIGH BRILLIANT 1995. SANTA BARBARA.   POT-SHOTS NO. 6776.

WHY DO I SUFFER THE SAME PAINFUL CONSEQUENCES,

Ashleigh Brilliant

EVERY TIME
I PERFORM
THE SAME
FOOLISH
ACTS?

© ASHLEIGH BRILLIANT 1998. SANTA BARBARA.   POT-SHOTS NO. 7706.

WHY CAN'T PEOPLE JUDGE ME BY MY OWN STANDARDS, AND NOT BY THEIRS?

Ashleigh Brilliant

© ASHLEIGH BRILLIANT 1993. SANTA BARBARA.

POT-SHOTS NO. 6224

Why do other people's mistakes amuse me so much more than my own?

Ashleigh Brilliant

© ASHLEIGH BRILLIANT 1995. SANTA BARBARA.

POT-SHOTS NO. 6801.

I HAD A GOOD REASON FOR HITTING HIM FIRST —

THE REASON IS THAT I'M UNCONTROLLABLY AGGRESSIVE.

Ashleigh Brilliant

© ASHLEIGH BRILLIANT 1996. SANTA BARBARA.

POT-SHOTS NO. 7354.

IT'S HARD TO BELIEVE YOU'RE TELLING THE TRUTH,

WHEN, IN YOUR PLACE I KNOW I'D BE LYING.

Ashleigh Brilliant

© ASHLEIGH BRILLIANT 1993. SANTA BARBARA.

POT-SHOTS NO. 6309.

THE BEST WAY I CAN HELP CERTAIN PEOPLE IS BY LETTING THEM FEEL SUPERIOR TO ME.

Ashleigh Brilliant

© ASHLEIGH BRILLIANT 1995. SANTA BARBARA

POT-SHOTS NO. 6822.

WHY ARE GOOD PEOPLE SO INTERESTED IN THE ACTIVITIES OF BAD PEOPLE?

Ashleigh Brilliant

© ASHLEIGH BRILLIANT 1996. SANTA BARBARA.

POT-SHOTS NO. 7520.

IF YOU MUST DO WHAT YOU KNOW IS SHAMEFUL, AT LEAST DON'T FORGET TO BE ASHAMED.

Ashleigh Brilliant

© ASHLEIGH BRILLIANT 1995.
SANTA BARBARA

POT-SHOTS NO. 6868.

OBVIOUSLY, THEY'RE NOT LIKE US ~

Ashleigh Brilliant

THE QUESTION IS, SHOULD WE WORSHIP THEM, OR ENSLAVE THEM?

© ASHLEIGH BRILLIANT 1993. SANTA BARBARA.

POT- SHOTS NO. 6341.

SOMEWHERE THERE OUGHT TO BE A PLACE

FOR PEOPLE WHO ALWAYS FEEL OUT OF PLACE.

Ashleigh Brilliant

© ASHLEIGH BRILLIANT 1998.

POT-SHOTS NO. 7545.

I'M ALWAYS ON YOUR SIDE ~

EVEN WHEN YOU'RE FIGHTING AGAINST YOURSELF.

Ashleigh Brilliant
SANTA BARBARA

All the Humanity   55

©ASHLEIGH BRILLIANT 1995. SANTA BARBARA.

POT-SHOTS NO. 6869.

EVERYBODY
HAS A RIGHT
TO LIVE ~

BUT NOT
NECESSARILY
TO
LIVE BETTER
THAN I DO.

Ashleigh Brilliant

©ASHLEIGH BRILLIANT 1993.

POT-SHOTS NO. 6546.

ACCORDING TO
EYEWITNESS
REPORTS,

NOBODY
SAW ANYTHING.

Ashleigh Brilliant
SANTA BARBARA

©ASHLEIGH BRILLIANT 1998
SANTA BARBARA.

POT-SHOTS NO. 7576.

*Ashleigh
Brilliant*

I TRY
TO TELL
EVERYONE
THE TRUTH ~

BUT
THAT DOESN'T
NECESSARILY
MEAN
TELLING EVERYONE
THE SAME THING.

© ASHLEIGH BRILLIANT 1993. SANTA BARBARA.

POT-SHOTS NO. 6549.

LET'S GET TOGETHER,

AND SEE THINGS MY WAY.

Ashleigh Brilliant

© ASHLEIGH BRILLIANT 1995.

POT-SHOTS NO. 6893.

SOME PEOPLE GET THEIR GREATEST SATISFACTION FROM HELPING OTHERS ~

OTHERS GET THEIRS FROM BEING HELPED.

Ashleigh Brilliant
SANTA BARBARA

© ASHLEIGH BRILLIANT 1995. SANTA BARBARA.

POT-SHOTS NO. 6727.

SOME PEOPLE WANT TO BE REMEMBERED,

SOME ARE REMEMBERED, WHETHER THEY WANT TO BE OR NOT.

Ashleigh Brilliant

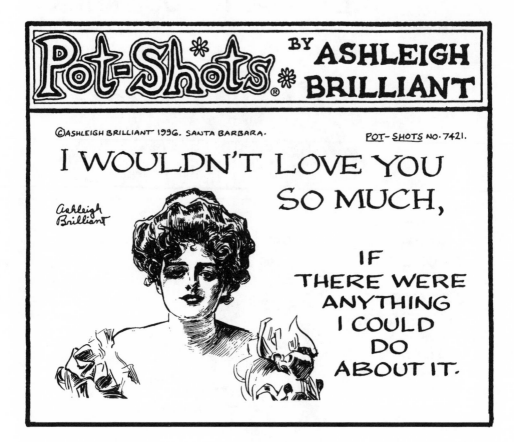

IV. Oh Pair

No Faith seems to be stronger than the kind TWO PEOPLE can have in each other, whether you want to call it love or friendship, or even loyal opposition. All over our planet, individuals who have trouble believing in anything else—even in themselves—fasten their faith on other individuals in intimate person-to-person relationships. Traditionally, the perpetuation of our species has been a by-product of many of these reciprocal fixations, but that situation is, of course, now rapidly changing. Thanks to artificial insemination and many other advances in technology, we can soon expect to see the total separation of reproduction from emotion, making it no longer biologically necessary for people to believe in each other at all.

In the meantime, however, we must continue to live in a world obsessed with human conjugation, and face the fact that almost every person one encounters is, was, or will be somebody else's "significant other"—perhaps even one's own. But being close in some ways often seems to precipitate divergence in others. Some people don't begin to discover who they really are until they become a member of a couple, and try to merge identities with the rest of the membership.

As this chapter will confirm, some of my most Brilliant Thoughts have arisen within the vortex of these closest human connections. Indeed, my hope is that in times of interpersonal turbulence, when there is clearly need to take cover, such messages may provide a kind of psychological storm-cellar.

© ASHLEIGH BRILLIANT 1998.
SANTA BARBARA

POT-SHOTS NO. 7809.

I CAN'T LIVE ENTIRELY ON YOUR HAPPINESS ~

I NEED TO HAVE A LITTLE OF MY OWN.

Ashleigh Brilliant

© ASHLEIGH BRILLIANT 1993. SANTA BARBARA.

POT-SHOTS NO. 6469.

I NEVER MISS YOU MORE THAN ALWAYS.

Ashleigh Brilliant

© ASHLEIGH BRILLIANT 1993. SANTA BARBARA.

POT-SHOTS NO. 6218.

DREAMS OCCUPY SO LITTLE SPACE,

SURELY THERE'S ROOM IN THE WORLD FOR BOTH YOURS AND MINE.

Ashleigh Brilliant

60

© ASHLEIGH BRILLIANT 1996.
SANTA BARBARA.

POT-SHOTS NO. 7487.

I CAN'T LOVE EVERYTHING YOU LOVE ~

SOMETIMES IT'S HARD ENOUGH JUST TO LOVE YOU.

Ashleigh Brilliant

© ASHLEIGH BRILLIANT 1998. SANTA BARBARA.

POT-SHOTS NO. 8142.

OUR RELATIONSHIP COULD GET YOU INTO A LOT OF TROUBLE,

BUT AREN'T I WORTH IT?

Ashleigh Brilliant

POT-SHOTS NO. 1685.

© ASHLEIGH BRILLIANT 1980.

WE'RE BOTH SO NICE,

DON'T WE DESERVE SOMETHING BETTER THAN EACH OTHER?

Ashleigh Brilliant

© ASHLEIGH BRILLIANT 1998. SANTA BARBARA.

POT-SHOTS NO. 7580.

IF WE CAN'T BE HAPPY TOGETHER,

AT LEAST LET ME COME AND BE SAD WITH YOU.

Ashleigh Brilliant

© BRILLIANT ENTERPRISES 1975.

POT-SHOTS NO. 817.

YOU KNOW I'LL ALWAYS STAY WITH YOU,

UNTIL I CAN'T BEAR IT ANY LONGER.

Ashleigh Brilliant

© ASHLEIGH BRILLIANT 1990. SANTA BARBARA

POT-SHOTS NO. 5024.

IN EVERY MARRIAGE, SOMEBODY HAS TO BE IN CHARGE

IN OUR MARRIAGE, IT'S THE CAT.

Ashleigh Brilliant

© ASHLEIGH BRILLIANT 1995, SANTA BARBARA POT-SHOTS NO. 6915.

One day
my love for you
will be
the oldest
living thing
in the universe.

Ashleigh Brilliant

© ASHLEIGH BRILLIANT 1998. SANTA BARBARA. POT-SHOTS NO. 7773.

LOVE MAY COME WHEN YOU'RE NOT EXPECTING IT ~

BUT IT'S
MORE LIKELY
TO COME
WHEN
YOU ARE.

Ashleigh Brilliant

© ASHLEIGH BRILLIANT 1992. POT-SHOTS NO. 5751.

IF THE WHOLE WORLD'S AGAINST ME, BUT YOU'RE ON MY SIDE,

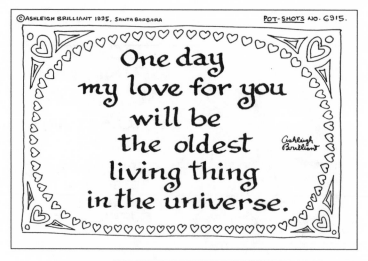

I'M
ALREADY
WINNING.

Ashleigh Brilliant
SANTA BARBARA

POT-SHOTS NO. 5803.

I AM SORRY FOR ANY INCONVENIENCE CAUSED BY THE FACT THAT I LOVE YOU.

© ASHLEIGH BRILLIANT 1992

Ashleigh Brilliant SANTA BARBARA

© ASHLEIGH BRILLIANT 1998. SANTA BARBARA

POT-SHOTS NO. 7589.

I COULD NEVER HAVE COME SO FAR

WITHOUT YOUR CONSTANT RESISTANCE.

Ashleigh Brilliant

© ASHLEIGH BRILLIANT 1995

POT-SHOTS NO. 6970.

THE CONDEMNED MAN'S WIFE

ATE A HEARTY BREAKFAST

Ashleigh Brilliant SANTA BARBARA

© ASHLEIGH BRILLIANT 1996. SANTA BARBARA.   POT-SHOTS NO. 7211.

THE STATISTICS ON HOW MUCH I LOVE YOU.

ARE STILL BEING COMPILED.

Ashleigh Brilliant

© ASHLEIGH BRILLIANT 1998. SANTA BARBARA.   POT-SHOTS NO. 7927.

THERE WAS A TIME WHEN MY TROUBLES WERE INCOMPLETE ~

THEN YOU CAME ALONG.

Ashleigh Brilliant

POT-SHOTS NO. 6159. © ASHLEIGH BRILLIANT 1993.

YOU AND I KNOW HOW MUCH YOU DISLIKE ME,

BUT CAN'T WE KEEP IT OUR SECRET?

Ashleigh Brilliant SANTA BARBARA.

Ashleigh Brilliant
SANTA BARBARA
©ASHLEIGH BRILLIANT 1996.   POT-SHOTS NO. 7285.

YOUR VIRTUES
BLIND ME
TO
YOUR FAULTS,

BUT ALAS,
ONLY IN
ONE EYE.

©ASHLEIGH BRILLIANT 1996. SANTA BARBARA.   POT-SHOTS NO. 7373.

YOU CAN
ALWAYS
RELY ON

MY
CONSTANT
UNSTEADINESS.

Ashleigh
Brilliant

©ASHLEIGH BRILLIANT 1993. SANTA BARBARA.   POT-SHOTS NO. 6181.

LET'S MAKE A RULE:

WE
NEEDN'T
TELL
EACH OTHER
EVERYTHING,

BUT
WHAT
WE DO TELL
IS TRUE.

Ashleigh Brilliant

© ASHLEIGH BRILLIANT 1998.   POT-SHOTS NO. 8016.

IF I DIDN'T KEEP MY EMOTIONS UNDER CONTROL,

THEY WOULD ALWAYS BE DRAGGING ME TOWARDS YOU.

POT-SHOTS NO. 8086.

IF YOU REALLY CAN'T IMPROVE,

I'LL JUST HAVE TO GO ON LOVING YOU THE WAY YOU ARE.

© ASHLEIGH BRILLIANT 1998. SANTA BARBARA.

© ASHLEIGH BRILLIANT 1998. SANTA BARBARA.   POT-SHOTS NO. 8104.

DON'T DISPOSE OF ME PERMANENTLY ~

SOMEDAY I MAY COME BACK INTO FASHION.

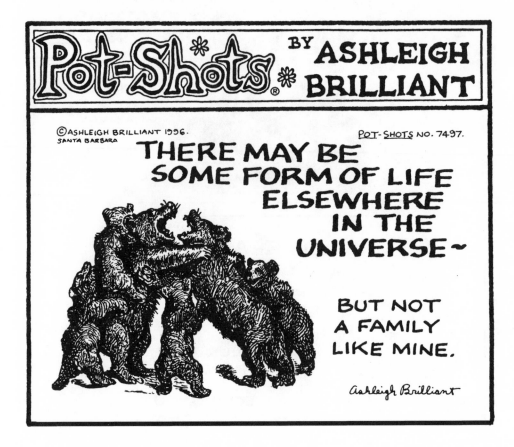

Pot-Shots ® BY ASHLEIGH BRILLIANT

© ASHLEIGH BRILLIANT 1996.
SANTA BARBARA

POT-SHOTS NO. 7497.

THERE MAY BE
SOME FORM OF LIFE
ELSEWHERE
IN THE
UNIVERSE~

BUT NOT
A FAMILY
LIKE MINE.

Ashleigh Brilliant

V. Family Portraits

When it comes to Faith, there is no more hallowed repository than the cluster of intimates we call a FAMILY. Whether we like them or not, we have to trust the people who most often encounter us with our defenses down. Anyone who has ever been part of such a group knows the sanctity which suffuses the bonds of kinship, and the special claims which are always somehow justified not by law, not by ethics, but by simple chemistry: the comparative densities of blood and water.

Like most other institutions, however, the family is changing. One can no longer assume that what is called a family unit will be founded upon any given pattern of marital, parental, or gender relationship. My own case, in fact, may now be considered rather exceptional. For better or worse, in my entire life, I have had just one male father, married to one female mother—and they never got divorced. Even more outlandish, I myself have so far had only one legal wife.

My other relatives have generally shunned the limelight, so I have found myself in the rather awkward position of being required to play the roles both of the pride of my family and of its black sheep. I fulfilled the first obligation by becoming a Doctor of Philosophy, and the second by becoming a purveyor of philosophically naughty postcards. Some products of the latter profession have been cajoled into appearing before you on the following pages. Please try to forgive any of these children of my mind who misbehave. I'm afraid such tendencies run in the family.

©ASHLEIGH BRILLIANT 1998. SANTA BARBARA. POT-SHOTS NO. 7700.

WHY MUST MARRYING JUST ONE PERSON

ALSO MEAN GETTING INVOLVED WITH SO MANY OTHER PEOPLE?

Ashleigh Brilliant

©ASHLEIGH BRILLIANT 1995. SANTA BARBARA. POT-SHOTS NO. 6819.

THE TROUBLE IS

THAT SEX IS A FORCE OF NATURE,

AND REASON IS NOT.

Ashleigh Brilliant

©ASHLEIGH BRILLIANT 1996. SANTA BARBARA. POT-SHOTS NO. 7297.

YOU MAY HAVE MARRIED THE RIGHT PERSON ~

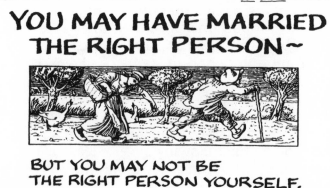

BUT YOU MAY NOT BE THE RIGHT PERSON YOURSELF.

Ashleigh Brilliant

©ASHLEIGH BRILLIANT 1998. SANTA BARBARA.

POT-SHOTS NO. 7829.

BEING A WIFE
(OR A HUSBAND)

CAN BE
ONE OF
THE LONELIEST
JOBS
IN THE WORLD.

Ashleigh Brilliant

POT-SHOTS NO. 6462.   ©ASHLEIGH BRILLIANT 1993.

I WISH
YOU HAD BEEN
A BETTER PARENT
TO ME,

AND I
A BETTER CHILD
TO YOU.

Ashleigh Brilliant SANTA BARBARA.

©ASHLEIGH BRILLIANT 1995.

POT-SHOTS NO. 6897.

PEOPLE WHO
ORGANIZE
BOOKS
BY
SUBJECT

SHOULD
NEVER
MARRY
PEOPLE
WHO
ARRANGE
THEM
BY
SIZE
AND
SHAPE.

Ashleigh Brilliant
SANTA
BARBARA

© ASHLEIGH BRILLIANT 1996

POT-SHOTS NO. 7115.

I LEARN SOMETHING NEW EVERY DAY ~

I LEARN WHAT IT'S LIKE TO BE A DAY OLDER.

Ashleigh Brilliant SANTA BARBARA

POT-SHOTS NO. 6912.

BEING A WOMAN

SHOULDN'T TAKE AS MUCH TIME AS IT DOES.

© ASHLEIGH BRILLIANT 1995

Ashleigh Brilliant SANTA BARBARA

Ashleigh Brilliant

POT-SHOTS NO. 2755.

IT'S HARD TO BELIEVE SOME GROWN-UPS WERE EVER CHILDREN,

AND THAT SOME CHILDREN WILL EVER GROW UP.

© ASHLEIGH BRILLIANT 1983.

© ASHLEIGH BRILLIANT 1996. SANTA BARBARA.

POT-SHOTS NO. 7459.

SOMEHOW I HAVE THE POWER TO BRIGHTEN THE WHOLE WORLD,

JUST BY PLEASING MY SPOUSE.

Ashleigh Brilliant

© ASHLEIGH BRILLIANT 1998. SANTA BARBARA.

POT-SHOTS NO. 8090.

THANK YOU FOR RUINING MY LIFE ~

IT WAS A GREAT EXPERIENCE.

Ashleigh Brilliant

POT-SHOTS NO. 2847.

Ashleigh Brilliant

NO MATTER HOW MANY TIMES I DO MY WORK,

IT NEVER STAYS DONE FOR LONG.

© ASHLEIGH BRILLIANT 1983.

© ASHLEIGH BRILLIANT, 1996. SANTA BARBARA.

The amount of love in just one mother's heart can supply the needs of an entire family.

© ASHLEIGH BRILLIANT 1996. SANTA BARBARA

WHY DO MARRIED PEOPLE

KEEP DISCOVERING MORE DIFFERENCES,

RATHER THAN

MORE SIMILARITIES?

Ashleigh Brilliant

© ASHLEIGH BRILLIANT 1998. SANTA BARBARA.

WHY AREN'T MY PARENTS MORE AWARE

OF ALL THE IMPORTANT THINGS I NEVER TELL THEM?

Ashleigh Brilliant

© ASHLEIGH BRILLIANT 1996. SANTA BARBARA.

POT-SHOTS NO. 7329.

SHE'S A PRETTY GOOD MOTHER,

FOR A WOMAN.

Ashleigh Brilliant

© ASHLEIGH BRILLIANT 1998.

POT-SHOTS NO. 7599.

IF YOU MUST MARRY,

TRY TO MARRY SOMEONE YOU CAN LIVE WITH.

Ashleigh Brilliant
SANTA BARBARA

© ASHLEIGH BRILLIANT 1993 SANTA BARBARA.

POT-SHOTS NO. 6198.

THERE WILL NEVER BE TRUE SOCIAL EQUALITY,

UNTIL MEN CAN DO EVERYTHING WOMEN CAN DO.

Ashleigh Brilliant

POT-SHOTS NO. 7175. ©ASHLEIGH BRILLIANT 1996.
SANTA BARBARA

PARENTS CAN
BE HARD
TO PLEASE ~

ESPECIALLY
WHEN YOU
HAVE TO START
BY DOING
WHAT THEY
WANT.

Ashleigh
Brilliant

POT-SHOTS NO. 1218.

Ashleigh
Brilliant
SANTA
BARBARA

WE TAKE
MY MOTHER
EVERYWHERE —

SHE'S ALMOST LIKE
ONE OF
THE FAMILY.

©BRILLIANT ENTERPRISES 1977.

©ASHLEIGH
BRILLIANT
1993.
SANTA BARBARA.

POT-SHOTS NO. 6364.

WHY
MUST
SO MANY
CHILDHOODS
CONTAIN
MATERIAL
WHICH IS
UNSUITABLE
FOR
CHILDREN?

Ashleigh Brilliant

78

© ASHLEIGH BRILLIANT 1996 · SANTA BARBARA.   POT-SHOTS NO. 7209.

COME HOME! ALL IS FORGOTTEN!

—IN FACT, WE CAN'T REMEMBER WHY YOU LEFT.

Ashleigh Brilliant

© ASHLEIGH BRILLIANT 1998·   POT-SHOTS NO. 7620.

WHEN SOMEONE I LOVE HURTS SOMEONE ELSE I LOVE,

THINK HOW IT HURTS ME!

Ashleigh Brilliant
SANTA BARBARA

© ASHLEIGH BRILLIANT 1998. SANTA BARBARA·   POT-SHOTS NO. 7781.

SOUNDS OF ANGUISH AND HOSTILITY!

—I MUST BE GETTING NEAR HOME.

Ashleigh Brilliant

© ASHLEIGH BRILLIANT 1996. SANTA BARBARA.   POT-SHOTS NO. 7217.

THE ONLY TIME YOU DON'T CARE WHAT PEOPLE THINK IS WHEN PEOPLE AGREE WITH ME.

Ashleigh Brilliant

© ASHLEIGH BRILLIANT 1998. SANTA BARBARA.   POT-SHOTS NO. 7759.

WHY CAN'T CHILDREN BE MORE UNDERSTANDING OF THE NEEDS OF PARENTS?

Ashleigh Brilliant

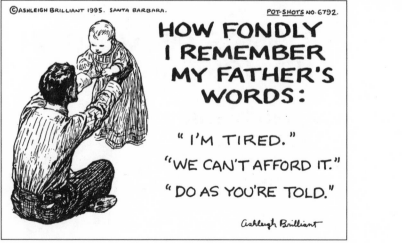

© ASHLEIGH BRILLIANT 1995. SANTA BARBARA.   POT-SHOTS NO. 6792.

HOW FONDLY I REMEMBER MY FATHER'S WORDS:

"I'M TIRED."

"WE CAN'T AFFORD IT."

"DO AS YOU'RE TOLD."

Ashleigh Brilliant

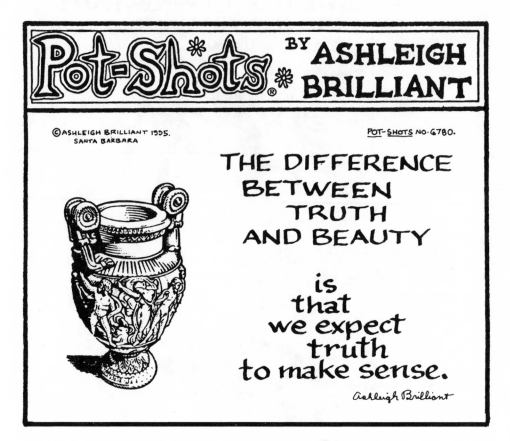

VI. Moments of Truth

Our quest for the truly believable now leads us to explore the country of TRUTH itself, that land which is also known to travelers coming from different directions by such other names as Reality, Knowledge, and the Universe. It's a complicated landscape, littered with the remains of old abandoned theories, full of stumbling-blocks and pitfalls.

I have always been suspicious of the Truth, ever since I discovered that even my own mother did not always tell it. I learned that there was a sort of monochrome scale which enabled certain lies to be considered "white," while others shaded off into varying degrees of darkness. "Reality" was even more suspect, especially since it seemed to be entirely at the mercy of our very gullible senses, and apparently switched off altogether every night, when a dramatically different regime called "dreaming" took over.

Still there are people who believe so devoutly in the Truth that the very word is holy to them. I used to attend a chess club which met at a local church, in a building whose acoustics were such that, whenever we were all sitting silently engrossed in our games, and somebody went to use the bathroom at the rear, every sound made therein was heard clearly by every other person present. Contending with this rather intrusive piece of Reality, I used to think of the name of that building, which was carved in large letters over its entrance: TRUTH HALL.

Certain portions of the Truth are indeed not always welcome, and the entire package really seems to be too much for anyone to handle. But I hope you'll find at least some of the following bite-sized morsels reasonably capable of ingestion.

©ASHLEIGH BRILLIANT 1998. SANTA BARBARA.

THE TRUTH IN A GOOD STORY

NEED NOT DEPEND ON

WHETHER OR NOT

IT EVER ACTUALLY HAPPENED.

Ashleigh Brilliant

©ASHLEIGH BRILLIANT 1995. SANTA BARBARA.

THE SECRET OF HAPPINESS IS TO ACCEPT REALITY,

BUT THEN PUT IT OUT OF YOUR MIND.

Ashleigh Brilliant

©ASHLEIGH BRILLIANT 1995. SANTA BARBARA.

I'M LOOKING FOR A FIELD OF STUDY

THAT DOESN'T REQUIRE ME TO REMEMBER ANYTHING.

Ashleigh Brilliant

© ASHLEIGH BRILLIANT 1998. SANTA BARBARA.

POT-SHOTS NO. 8074.

THERE'S A VERY REAL POSSIBILITY

THAT NOTHING AT ALL IS REAL.

© ASHLEIGH BRILLIANT 1995. SANTA BARBARA.

POT-SHOTS NO. 6856.

I HAVEN'T TIME FOR ALL THE DETAILS ~

JUST TELL ME THE ULTIMATE PURPOSE OF THE UNIVERSE.

© ASHLEIGH BRILLIANT 1996. SANTA BARBARA

POT-SHOTS NO. 7504.

I KNOW WHAT REALITY IS~

I'VE BEEN THERE — I DIDN'T LIKE IT.

© ASHLEIGH BRILLIANT 1990.   POT-SHOTS NO. 5023.

IT'S HARD TO KNOW
EXACTLY WHICH WAY
TO TURN

IN ORDER
TO FACE
REALITY.

Ashleigh Brilliant
SANTA BARBARA

© ASHLEIGH BRILLIANT 1982.   POT-SHOTS NO. 2446.

If you
tire
of your
dreams,

REALITY
IS ALWAYS
AVAILABLE
AT NO
EXTRA
CHARGE.

Ashleigh Brilliant

© ASHLEIGH BRILLIANT 1996.   POT-SHOTS NO. 7525.
SANTA
BARBARA

WHY CAN'T
KNOWLEDGE
BE
INHERITED?

WHY MUST
EACH NEW
GENERATION
LEARN
THE SAME THINGS
ALL OVER AGAIN?

Ashleigh
Brilliant

© ASHLEIGH BRILLIANT 1991.   POT-SHOTS NO. 5519.

GOOD READING CAN BE VERY INSPIRING ~

it always inspires me to do more reading.

© ASHLEIGH BRILLIANT 1996.   POT-SHOTS NO. 7062.
SANTA BARBARA

MY BEAUTIFUL FANTASIES FLOAT ON A SEA OF REALITY ~

THE PROBLEM IS TO PREVENT LEAKS.

© ASHLEIGH BRILLIANT 1998   POT-SHOTS NO. 7547.

THE FIRST RULE OF DREAMING

IS THAT DREAMS ARE NOT BOUND BY ANY RULES.

Ashleigh Brilliant
SANTA BARBARA

© ASHLEIGH BRILLIANT 1996. SANTA BARBARA

POT-SHOTS NO. 7061.

DON'T READ TOO MANY BOOKS,

OR YOU'LL BEGIN TO THINK YOU KNOW NOTHING AT ALL.

Ashleigh Brilliant

© ASHLEIGH BRILLIANT 1992. SANTA BARBARA.

POT-SHOTS NO. 5961.

DON'T FACE REALITY~

IT'S TERRIBLY DISAPPOINTING.

Ashleigh Brilliant

© ASHLEIGH BRILLIANT 1998. SANTA BARBARA.

POT-SHOTS NO. 7578.

WHEN IT'S MY FAITH AGAINST YOUR STATISTICS,

YOUR STATISTICS HAVEN'T GOT A CHANCE.

Ashleigh Brilliant

POT-SHOTS NO. 6105 ©ASHLEIGH BRILLIANT 1993.

IN MY DREAMS, I'M ALWAYS TRAVELLING ~

EXCEPT WHEN I'M REALLY TRAVELLING ~

THEN, I DREAM I'M AT HOME.

Ashleigh Brilliant
SANTA BARBARA

©ASHLEIGH BRILLIANT 1996.
SANTA BARBARA

POT-SHOTS NO. 7083.

ISN'T THERE ANYTHING TOO BAD TO BE TRUE?

Ashleigh Brilliant

©ASHLEIGH BRILLIANT 1998 · SANTA BARBARA.

POT-SHOTS NO. 7680.

Ashleigh Brilliant

ART

IS WHAT BECOMES OF REALITY AFTER IT HAS PASSED THROUGH AN ARTIST.

© ASHLEIGH BRILLIANT 1993. *Ashleigh Brilliant* POT-SHOTS NO. 6108.
SANTA BARBARA.

WHAT DOESN'T SEEM TO FIT THE PATTERN

MAY BE PART OF A LARGER PATTERN WE DON'T SEE.

© ASHLEIGH BRILLIANT 1996. POT-SHOTS NO. 7159.

I DIDN'T HEAR THE QUESTION ~

BUT THE ANSWER IS PROBABLY:

Ashleigh Brilliant

I DON'T KNOW.

© ASHLEIGH BRILLIANT 1998 · SANTA BARBARA. POT-SHOTS NO. 7768.
Ashleigh Brilliant

THE FACTS MAY BE AGAINST ME,

but all the illusions are on my side.

© ASHLEIGH BRILLIANT 1996. SANTA BARBARA.

POT-SHOTS NO. 7176.

NO PASSPORT

IS MORE VALUABLE THAN YOUR LIBRARY CARD.

Ashleigh Brilliant

© ASHLEIGH BRILLIANT 1998. SANTA BARBARA.

POT-SHOTS NO. 7857.

THE ALLEGED SIZE OF THE UNIVERSE DOESN'T IMPRESS ME ~

I'M SURE ALL THE FIGURES HAVE BEEN EXAGGERATED.

Ashleigh Brilliant

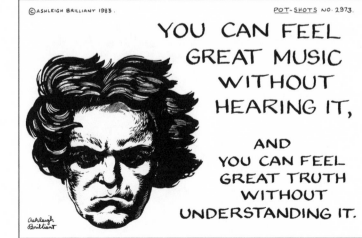

© ASHLEIGH BRILLIANT 1983.

POT-SHOTS NO. 2973.

YOU CAN FEEL GREAT MUSIC WITHOUT HEARING IT,

AND YOU CAN FEEL GREAT TRUTH WITHOUT UNDERSTANDING IT.

Ashleigh Brilliant

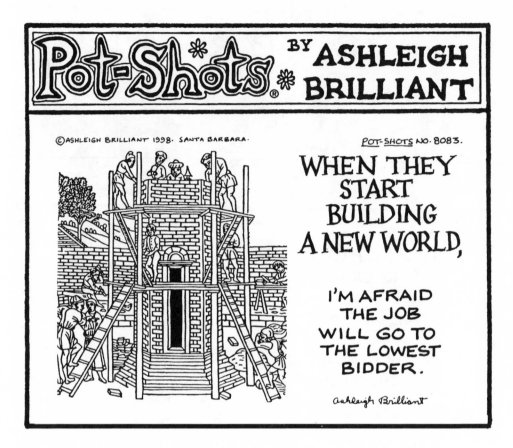

POT-SHOTS NO. 8083.

WHEN THEY START BUILDING A NEW WORLD,

I'M AFRAID THE JOB WILL GO TO THE LOWEST BIDDER.

Ashleigh Brilliant

©ASHLEIGH BRILLIANT 1998. SANTA BARBARA.

VII. Whirled Without End

You don't have to save all your Faith for the Next World. You can actually start believing in this one. It's called idealism—and Justice, Peace, Freedom, Patriotism, and Progress are some of its most fervently followed creeds. The affairs of THIS WORLD may not have all the glamour of regions farther afield, but they do, for many of us, offer the advantage of greater accessibility, and more of a chance to participate personally, if only, sometimes, as a victim.

Vital issues, great movements, momentous events, march relentlessly across our information screens, and now and then even register on our minds. Often the action seems far away—but, living as we do on the surface of a sphere, we all have (at least geometrically) an equal claim to be at the real center of things. My wife Dorothy, for whom Travel (see Chapter 10) is only one of many Earthly Gods (others include Figure Skating, Cats, and Hamburgers), has made a collection of maps of the World, published in different countries she has visited—and each map shows its own country right in the middle.

But no matter how we view our position in it, This World is likely to be around for some time yet, and therefore ought to be kept as habitable as possible, especially since no other known world appears to be as people-friendly. Our leaders are supposedly aware of this need, but let's be fair—many other matters besides human survival are competing for their attention.

Weighty considerations such as these loom over the present chapter, but should not be permitted to interfere with anything less ponderous you had planned for today. After all, what's the point of surviving if we're not also, at least occasionally, having a good time?

© ASHLEIGH BRILLIANT 1996. SANTA BARBARA.

POT-SHOTS NO. 7404.

THERE'S A WORD FOR HOPE IN EVERY LANGUAGE ~

AT LEAST, I HOPE THERE IS.

Ashleigh Brilliant

© ASHLEIGH BRILLIANT 1995.

POT-SHOTS NO. 6904.

WHY CAN'T THOSE IN THE RIGHT ALWAYS BE AS UNITED AND DETERMINED

Ashleigh Brilliant SANTA BARBARA

AS THOSE IN THE WRONG?

© ASHLEIGH BRILLIANT 1996. SANTA BARBARA.

POT-SHOTS NO. 7511.

MACHINES ARE BECOMING MORE LIKE PEOPLE,

TO SAVE PEOPLE FROM BECOMING MORE LIKE MACHINES.

Ashleigh Brilliant

© ASHLEIGH BRILLIANT 1998. SANTA BARBARA.

POT-SHOTS NO. 8144.

HOW MANY PEOPLE NOT WANTING WAR

DOES IT REQUIRE FOR WAR NOT TO HAPPEN?

Ashleigh Brilliant

© ASHLEIGH BRILLIANT 1988.

POT-SHOTS NO. 4384

THERE OUGHT TO BE A LAW AGAINST

TOO MANY RULES AND REGULATIONS.

Ashleigh Brilliant

© ASHLEIGH BRILLIANT 1996.

POT-SHOTS NO. 7041.

PEOPLE DO GET TIRED OF KILLING~

Ashleigh Brilliant SANTA BARBARA

BUT THEY ALSO SEEM TO GET TIRED OF NOT KILLING.

© ASHLEIGH BRILLIANT 1996. POT-SHOTS NO. 7521.

HISTORY TEACHES

THAT HAVING
THE WHOLE WORLD
AGAINST YOU

DOESN'T
NECESSARILY
MEAN
YOU WILL LOSE.

Ashleigh Brilliant
SANTA BARBARA

© ASHLEIGH BRILLIANT 1998. SANTA BARBARA. POT-SHOTS NO. 8145.

YOU CAN GET JUSTICE
IF YOU CAN
PAY FOR IT ~

~ BUT IS THAT
REALLY
JUSTICE?

Ashleigh Brilliant

© ASHLEIGH BRILLIANT 1993. SANTA BARBARA. POT-SHOTS NO. 6521.

GIVE THE PEOPLE
WHAT THEY
WANT ~

BUT FIRST
MAKE THEM
WANT
WHAT THEY
REALLY
OUGHT TO HAVE.

Ashleigh Brilliant

© ASHLEIGH BRILLIANT 1996. SANTA BARBARA.

POT-SHOTS NO. 7092.

IT'S NOT SURPRISING THERE'S SO MUCH TROUBLE,

IN A WORLD WHICH IS FULL OF FOREIGNERS.

Ashleigh Brilliant

© ASHLEIGH BRILLIANT 1998.

POT-SHOTS NO. 7632.

THE GREATEST LEADERS

ARE THOSE WHO KNOW WHEN IT'S TIME TO CHANGE DIRECTION.

Ashleigh Brilliant
SANTA BARBARA

© ASHLEIGH BRILLIANT 1995. SANTA BARBARA.

POT-SHOTS NO. 6618.

TRY TO BE ON THE SIDE OF THE POLICE,

EVEN WHEN IT'S UNCLEAR WHOSE SIDE THEY'RE ON.

Ashleigh Brilliant

© ASHLEIGH BRILLIANT 1996.
SANTA BARBARA

POT-SHOTS NO. 7100.

IN A SOCIETY
SUPPOSEDLY
BASED ON
EQUALITY,

IS IT FAIR
THAT
MOST CRIMINALS
ARE STILL MEN?

Ashleigh Brilliant

© ASHLEIGH BRILLIANT 1998. SANTA BARBARA.

POT-SHOTS NO. 7719.

WHY DOES LITTER
COST SO MUCH
TO COLLECT,

WHEN
IT GETS
DISTRIBUTED
FOR NOTHING?

Ashleigh Brilliant

© ASHLEIGH BRILLIANT 1995. SANTA BARBARA. Ashleigh Brilliant

POT-SHOTS NO. 6659.

BEING
A LEADER
DOESN'T
MEAN
ALWAYS
BEING
RIGHT —

BUT IT DOES MEAN
TAKING
RESPONSIBILITY
FOR BEING WRONG.

© ASHLEIGH BRILLIANT 1996. SANTA BARBARA.

POT-SHOTS NO. 7101

THERE ARE WORSE THINGS THAN NOISE ~ BUT I CAN'T THINK OF ANY, BECAUSE OF ALL THE NOISE.

Ashleigh Brilliant

© ASHLEIGH BRILLIANT 1998 SANTA BARBARA.

POT-SHOTS NO. 7841.

PEOPLE WHO DON'T BELIEVE IN PROGRESS MUST HAVE FORGOTTEN HOW BAD THINGS USED TO BE.

Ashleigh Brilliant

© ASHLEIGH BRILLIANT 1995.

POT-SHOTS NO. 6707.

MY COMPUTER HAS NO FEELINGS, BUT I HAVE MORE THAN ENOUGH FOR THE TWO OF US.

Ashleigh Brilliant
SANTA BARBARA

© ASHLEIGH BRILLIANT 1996. SANTA BARBARA.

POT-SHOTS NO. 7109.

MOST PEOPLE DON'T LIKE TO COMPLAIN ~

Ashleigh Brilliant

THAT'S WHY
THERE'S STILL
SO MUCH
EVIL
IN THE WORLD.

© ASHLEIGH BRILLIANT 1998. SANTA BARBARA.

POT-SHOTS NO. 7954.

IN MY IDEAL COMMUNITY,

PEOPLE ARE
CONCERNED ABOUT
EACH OTHER,

BUT THEY
ALSO MIND THEIR
OWN BUSINESS.

Ashleigh Brilliant

© ASHLEIGH BRILLIANT 1995. SANTA BARBARA.

POT-SHOTS NO. 6803.

BEFORE THERE WERE NEWS MEDIA,

Ashleigh Brilliant

HOW
DID PEOPLE
KNOW
WHAT TO
WORRY ABOUT?

102

© ASHLEIGH BRILLIANT 1996. SANTA BARBARA.

POT-SHOTS NO. 7276.

DON'T EXPECT ANY PUBLIC SERVICE AWARDS

FOR HAVING MORE CHILDREN

IN AN OVER-POPULATED WORLD.

Ashleigh Brilliant

© ASHLEIGH BRILLIANT 1998. SANTA BARBARA

POT-SHOTS NO. 8043.

LAY DOWN MORE CONCRETE!~

I CAN STILL SEE A TREE.

Ashleigh Brilliant

© ASHLEIGH BRILLIANT 1995. SANTA BARBARA.

POT-SHOTS NO. 6825.

DON'T CALL IT FREEDOM,

UNLESS IT INCLUDES THE FREEDOM TO BE

ABSOLUTELY DISGUSTING

Ashleigh Brilliant

© ASHLEIGH BRILLIANT 1996.
SANTA BARBARA

POT-SHOTS NO. 7447.

THERE'S NEVER A GOOD REASON FOR INJUSTICE ~

BUT NOT EVERYTHING IN LIFE HAPPENS FOR A GOOD REASON.

© ASHLEIGH BRILLIANT 1998.
SANTA BARBARA

POT-SHOTS NO. 8105.

THE VOICE OF THE PEOPLE IS LOUD AND CLEAR ~

IT SAYS "PLEASE ALLOW ME TO REMAIN SILENT."

Ashleigh Brilliant

© ASHLEIGH BRILLIANT 1996.

POT-SHOTS NO. 7312.

HOW DO I KNOW THE WORLD WON'T STOP WHEN I DO?

Ashleigh Brilliant
SANTA BARBARA

Whirled Without End

VIII. Souled Out

If This World doesn't give you enough to believe in, there is always the HEREAFTER, a place notoriously dependent upon Faith for its very existence. What happens to people when they die? Most of us don't concern ourselves about the postmortem prospects of termites or cockroaches. (If we did, the pesticide industry would have to do some deep soul-searching.) But when it comes to people, and especially people close to us, well that's another story. And when it comes to the closest person of all—the good old Self—that indeed is another whole chapter—this chapter, in fact.

Let's face it—this particular question, and the fact that we do all have to face it, is actually the greatest thing we all have in common. That (no doubt) is one reason why human beings, as a class, are frequently referred to in literature as "mortals." As a paid-up mortal in good standing since 1933, I am, like most of the rest of us, anxious to maintain that status as long as possible. Not that I have anything against immortality per se—but I can't help having doubts about the exact process by which it is to be achieved.

About my work, however, I have fewer qualms. If any part of it, after having been born in my mind, passes over into yours, surely to that extent we are both already tasting the immortality of a Brilliant Thought.

© ASHLEIGH BRILLIANT 1995.
SANTA BARBARA

POT-SHOTS NO. 6665.

DON'T ASK ME WHAT HAPPENS AFTER DEATH~

I'M NOT
EVEN SURE
WHAT HAPPENS
AFTER DINNER.

Ashleigh Brilliant

© ASHLEIGH BRILLIANT 1995.

POT-SHOTS NO. 6953.

Ashleigh
Brilliant
SANTA BARBARA

EXISTENCE IS A VERY STRANGE THING ~

— FIRST
YOU AREN'T,
THEN YOU ARE,
THEN
YOU AREN'T AGAIN.

POT-SHOTS NO. 6456.

THE CLOSEST I'VE EVER BEEN TO DEATH

Ashleigh
Brilliant

WAS
BEFORE
I WAS BORN.

© ASHLEIGH BRILLIANT 1993. SANTA BARBARA.

108

POT-SHOTS NO. 7892.

IF I DON'T DO IT BEFORE I DIE,

I'M NOT SURE I'LL EVER DO IT AT ALL.

©ASHLEIGH BRILLIANT 1998.

Ashleigh Brilliant
SANTA BARBARA

©ASHLEIGH BRILLIANT 1991.

POT-SHOTS NO. 5534.

Ashleigh Brilliant
SANTA BARBARA

IT'S RIDICULOUS AND ILLOGICAL

FOR A LIVING PERSON

TO WORRY ABOUT BEING DEAD ~

(YET ALSO QUITE NATURAL).

©ASHLEIGH BRILLIANT 1996.
SANTA BARBARA

POT-SHOTS NO. 7027.

IF DYING MEANS DEPARTING,

LIFE IS REALLY JUST A LONG GOING-AWAY PARTY.

Ashleigh Brilliant

© ASHLEIGH BRILLIANT 1996. SANTA BARBARA.   POT-SHOTS NO. 7319.

MOST DREAMS END WHEN YOU WAKE ~

BUT WHEN
THE DREAM OF LIFE ENDS,
YOU GO TO SLEEP.

Ashleigh Brilliant

© ASHLEIGH BRILLIANT 1998. SANTA BARBARA.   POT-SHOTS NO. 7901.

I HOPE
I REMEMBER
ENOUGH
OF THIS WORLD
IN THE NEXT ONE

TO APPRECIATE THE CHANGE.

Ashleigh Brilliant

© ASHLEIGH BRILLIANT 1993. SANTA BARBARA.   POT-SHOTS NO. 6274.

I HAVEN'T YET LIVED FOREVER ~

BUT AT LEAST
I'VE
MADE
A
START.

Ashleigh Brilliant

110

© ASHLEIGH BRILLIANT 1996. SANTA BARBARA.

POT-SHOTS NO 7496.

IN THE PRISON OF THIS WORLD,

EVERYBODY GETS A LIFE SENTENCE,

FOLLOWED BY A DEATH SENTENCE.

Ashleigh Brilliant

© ASHLEIGH BRILLIANT 1996. SANTA BARBARA

POT-SHOTS NO. 7110.

Ashleigh Brilliant

EVERY DAY BRINGS ME CLOSER TO MY JOURNEY'S END,

AND TO MY NEXT JOURNEY'S BEGINNING.

© ASHLEIGH BRILLIANT 1996. SANTA BARBARA.

POT-SHOTS NO. 7229.

Ashleigh Brilliant

IF YOU'VE ALWAYS LIVED IN A TUNNEL,

NOTHING IS MORE FRIGHTENING THAN THE LIGHT AT THE END.

© ASHLEIGH BRILLIANT 1996. SANTA BARBARA.

POT-SHOTS NO. 7166.

I'VE GOT TO KEEP GOING HERE,

UNTIL PROPER ARRANGEMENTS ARE MADE FOR ME

IN THE NEXT LIFE.

Ashleigh Brilliant

© ASHLEIGH BRILLIANT 1996. SANTA BARBARA

POT-SHOTS NO. 7522.

I FIND MYSELF IN A STRANGE SITUATION —

SOMEWHERE BETWEEN TWO ETERNITIES,

ON AN ISLAND CALLED LIFE.

Ashleigh Brilliant

© ASHLEIGH BRILLIANT 1993.

POT-SHOTS NO. 6507.

DEATH ISN'T NECESSARILY HOW I'D CHOOSE TO END MY LIFE ~

but no other options are currently available.

Ashleigh Brilliant
SANTA BARBARA

© ASHLEIGH BRILLIANT 1996   POT-SHOTS NO. 7177.

I CAN ONLY HOPE

MY LIFE IS GOOD PREPARATION

FOR WHATEVER COMES NEXT.

Ashleigh Brilliant
SANTA BARBARA

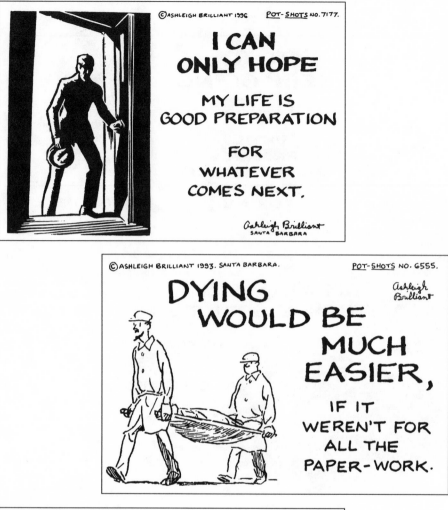

© ASHLEIGH BRILLIANT 1993. SANTA BARBARA.   POT-SHOTS NO. 6555.

Ashleigh Brilliant

DYING WOULD BE MUCH EASIER,

IF IT WEREN'T FOR ALL THE PAPER-WORK.

© ASHLEIGH BRILLIANT 1996.
SANTA BARBARA   POT-SHOTS NO. 7194.

IF IT'S BETTER NOT TO BE THAN TO BE,

WE ALL HAVE PLENTY TO LOOK FORWARD TO.

Ashleigh Brilliant

© ASHLEIGH BRILLIANT 1998 SANTA BARBARA

POT-SHOTS NO. 7571

IF YOU REALLY WANT IMMORTALITY,

YOU'VE GOT TO BE WILLING TO DIE FOR IT.

Ashleigh Brilliant

© ASHLEIGH BRILLIANT 1998.

POT-SHOTS NO. 7650.

AFTER I DIE,

I WILL AT LEAST HAVE ONE LESS THING TO WORRY ABOUT.

Ashleigh Brilliant
SANTA BARBARA

© ASHLEIGH BRILLIANT 1996. SANTA BARBARA.

POT-SHOTS NO. 7210.

I'LL MAKE FEWER MISTAKES IN MY NEXT LIFE ~

UNLESS I'M MISTAKEN IN EXPECTING ANOTHER LIFE.

Ashleigh Brilliant

©ASHLEIGH BRILLIANT 1998.
SANTA BARBARA

POT-SHOTS NO. 7807.

MY PLAN IS NOT TO DIE ~

IF THAT DOESN'T WORK, I'LL HAVE TO TRY SOMETHING ELSE.

Ashleigh Brilliant

©ASHLEIGH BRILLIANT 1995.

POT-SHOTS NO. 6865.

LOOK AT IT THIS WAY:

NO MATTER WHERE YOU GO WHEN YOU DIE,

ALL EXPENSES ARE PAID.

Ashleigh Brilliant
SANTA BARBARA

©ASHLEIGH BRILLIANT 1996.

POT-SHOTS NO. 7222.

IT'S VERY HARD TO DENY DEATH ALTOGETHER ~

BUT CAN'T I AT LEAST HAVE SOME DOUBTS ABOUT IT?

Ashleigh Brilliant
SANTA BARBARA

Pot-Shots® BY ASHLEIGH BRILLIANT

©ASHLEIGH BRILLIANT 1996. SANTA BARBARA.

POT-SHOTS NO. 7342.

WHY DOES GOD PUT US IN SUCH A BIG SPACE,

BUT GIVE US SO LITTLE TIME?

Ashleigh Brilliant

IX. Oddly Godly

At this point, we stop beating about the burning bush, and plunge head-first into MATTERS THEOLOGICAL. You can believe in other things until you're blue in the face—it won't make a scrap of difference to your spiritual health, until you latch on to some Topmost Level of Authority in the Universe, where the Buck not only truly stops, but where it started in the first place.

Choosing your own god is a process so difficult that, to bypass it, the whole concept of ready-made religion was invented. Religion as a package not only gives you a pre-assembled god, but also a code of conduct, a collection of holy places and objects, and a set of more or less satisfying answers to some of life's most bothersome questions.

My own religious education began in the first grade of a Toronto public school, where in those days it was not thought improper to have readings by the teacher from the earlier sections of the Bible. But I was somewhat skeptical from the start. I remember wondering, upon hearing about the Children of Israel "worshipping in the desert," how those warships ever got into the desert.

Since then, I have been exposed to a variety of persuasions, without ever coming very close to being persuaded. I have learned, however, that it is possible to admire, respect, sometimes even envy, the believer, without being able to buy the belief. The alternative has been to propagate a gospel of my own, which (compared with most of the others) at least possesses the virtue of not taking itself too seriously. As to what chances there may be of any truly mystical insights emerging from your study of these works of mine, I can only say, God knows!

©ASHLEIGH BRILLIANT 1996. SANTA BARBARA.

POT-SHOTS NO. 7413.

I DO BELIEVE IN SOME KIND OF GOD,

BUT HAVEN'T YET WORKED OUT ALL THE DETAILS.

Ashleigh Brilliant

©ASHLEIGH BRILLIANT 1996. SANTA BARBARA

POT-SHOTS NO. 7026.

IN MY RELIGION,

I DON'T ASK, AND GOD DOESN'T TELL.

Ashleigh Brilliant

©ASHLEIGH BRILLIANT 1996.

POT-SHOTS NO. 7466.

MY AGREEMENT WITH GOD

says he'll compensate me somewhere else for everything he does to me here.

Ashleigh Brilliant
SANTA BARBARA

120

© ASHLEIGH BRILLIANT 1998.

Ashleigh Brilliant
SANTA BARBARA

POT-SHOTS NO. 7791.

PEOPLE WHO SEND ME MONEY

MAY VERY POSSIBLY BE IMPROVING THEIR CHANCES OF GETTING INTO HEAVEN.

POT-SHOTS NO. 6058.

ONE DAY I MAY RETURN TO GOD ~

IF GOD IS STILL THERE.

© ASHLEIGH BRILLIANT 1992.

Ashleigh Brilliant
SANTA BARBARA

© ASHLEIGH BRILLIANT 1996.
SANTA BARBARA

POT-SHOTS NO. 7054.

HERE'S A GOOD RECIPE FOR INSANITY:

KEEP TRYING TO ANSWER QUESTIONS WHICH YOU KNOW ARE UNANSWERABLE.

Ashleigh Brilliant

© ASHLEIGH BRILLIANT 1998. SANTA BARBARA.

POT-SHOTS NO. 7546.

WIN A FREE TRIP TO HEAVEN!

DETAILS AT YOUR LOCAL HOUSE OF WORSHIP.

Ashleigh Brilliant

© ASHLEIGH BRILLIANT 1998. SANTA BARBARA

POT-SHOTS NO. 7800.

I CAN'T DETECT ANY LONG-TERM PLAN~

THE UNIVERSE SEEMS TO OPERATE STRICTLY ON A DAY-TO-DAY BASIS.

Ashleigh Brilliant

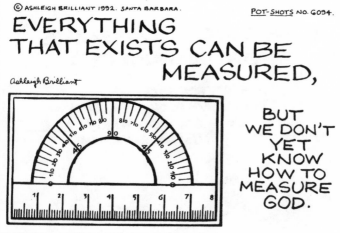

© ASHLEIGH BRILLIANT 1992. SANTA BARBARA.

POT-SHOTS NO. 6094.

EVERYTHING THAT EXISTS CAN BE MEASURED,

Ashleigh Brilliant

BUT WE DON'T YET KNOW HOW TO MEASURE GOD.

© ASHLEIGH BRILLIANT 1996.
SANTA BARBARA

POT-SHOTS NO. 7124.

IF GOD REALLY IS DEAD,

IT MUST HAVE BEEN SUICIDE.

Ashleigh Brilliant

© ASHLEIGH BRILLIANT 1998. SANTA BARBARA.

POT-SHOTS NO. 7598.

FINDING GOD

WOULD BE HARD ENOUGH,

EVEN IF HE DIDN'T GO UNDER SO MANY DIFFERENT NAMES.

Ashleigh Brilliant

POT-SHOTS NO. 6173.

PAIN IS NO JOKE

OR, IF IT IS, GOD HAS A VERY STRANGE SENSE OF HUMOR.

Ashleigh Brilliant
SANTA BARBARA.

© ASHLEIGH BRILLIANT 1993.

© ASHLEIGH BRILLIANT 1996.   POT-SHOTS NO. 7167.

Ashleigh Brilliant
SANTA BARBARA

Surely God doesn't do all these wonderful things just to impress us.

© ASHLEIGH BRILLIANT 1998.   POT-SHOTS NO. 7617.

NOBODY

KNOWS WHAT GOD WILL DO NEXT —

(PERHAPS NOT EVEN GOD).

Ashleigh Brilliant
SANTA BARBARA

© ASHLEIGH BRILLIANT 1993. SANTA BARBARA.   POT-SHOTS NO. 6579.

WHAT MAKES SOME PEOPLE NEED A HOPE OF HEAVEN,

Ashleigh Brilliant

WHILE OTHERS CAN BE HAPPY EVEN WITHOUT ONE?

© ASHLEIGH BRILLIANT 1996 · SANTA BARBARA.   POT-SHOTS NO. 7241.

GOD IS SO NICE,

I ALMOST WISH THERE WERE MORE THAN ONE.

Ashleigh Brilliant

© ASHLEIGH BRILLIANT 1998 · SANTA BARBARA.   POT-SHOTS NO. 7621.

DESPITE MANY EXPERIMENTS,

no one form of prayer

has yet been proven

more effective than any other.

Ashleigh Brilliant

POT-SHOTS NO. G448

BELIEVING IN GOOD THINGS DOESN'T MAKE THEM TRUE,

BUT GIVES YOU A HAPPIER LIFE IN THE MEANTIME.

© ASHLEIGH BRILLIANT 1995.   *Ashleigh Brilliant* SANTA BARBARA

© ASHLEIGH BRILLIANT 1998. SANTA BARBARA.

POT-SHOTS NO. 7628

THERE MUST BE A HEAVEN ~

OR A LOT OF PEOPLE ARE GOING TO BE VERY DISAPPOINTED.

Ashleigh Brilliant

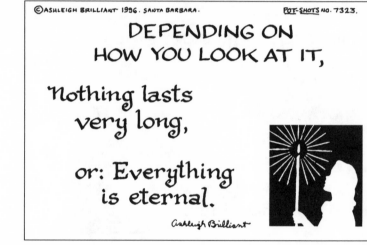

© ASHLEIGH BRILLIANT 1996. SANTA BARBARA.

POT-SHOTS NO. 7323.

DEPENDING ON HOW YOU LOOK AT IT,

Nothing lasts very long,

or: Everything is eternal.

Ashleigh Brilliant

© ASHLEIGH BRILLIANT 1993. SANTA BARBARA.

POT-SHOTS NO. 6581.

MY FAVORITE COMMANDMENTS

ARE THOSE THAT PROHIBIT WHAT I HAVE NO INTEREST IN DOING ANYWAY.

Ashleigh Brilliant

©ASHLEIGH BRILLIANT 1996. SANTA BARBARA.

TRY TO GET SOME PLEASURE OUT OF LIFE ~

Ashleigh Brilliant

(UNLESS IT'S FORBIDDEN BY YOUR RELIGION).

©ASHLEIGH BRILLIANT 1998.

IN GOD'S CASINO,

THE HOUSE ALWAYS WINS.

Ashleigh Brilliant
SANTA BARBARA

©ASHLEIGH BRILLIANT 1995.
SANTA BARBARA

THE GREAT RELIGIONS ALL AGREE

Ashleigh Brilliant

that what really matters isn't what you believe,

but how you live.

X. Diverse Devotions

Seek under the rubric of Faith, and you will find a vast variety of piety. *Laborare est orare,* said the Romans: "To work is to pray." This Chapter finds devotional activity not only in WORK, but also in TRAVEL (a word derived, we must remember, from "travail"), and in the whole process of working our way through Life.

If prayer is really the most meaningful way of spending one's time, I suppose there are many people for whom to watch TV, or to make love, or even to fight or to gamble, is to pray. For me, it would have to be to write, or to eat—which would necessarily give some kind of holy status in my own personal pantheon to my Publisher and my Grocer. But why should our communing with the Infinite require any special activity at all? Surely the Infinite is already perfectly (or, if you like, Infinitely) aware of everything we could possibly want to communicate.

Be that as it may, prayer, even the conventional kind, remains a popular, and, in most societies, a socially-approved, activity. Controversies do however periodically erupt concerning the time, place, and manner in which it is performed. For example, in America, as a general rule, it has been found better not to pray in such a way as to interfere with business, or to require summoning of the Fire Department or the Vice Squad.

Religious freedom does seem to have become more widespread in recent times—but perhaps only because people no longer consider such matters as important as in the good old days, when a debate over how many angels could dance on the head of a pin might trigger widespread violence. (For what it's worth, I personally have always felt that one angel per pin would be quite enough.)

© ASHLEIGH BRILLIANT 1995 POT-SHOTS NO. 6889.

THE LAST PART OF LIFE
OUGHT
TO BE
THE
BEST
PART~

WHY
ISN'T IT?

Ashleigh Brilliant
SANTA BARBARA

© ASHLEIGH BRILLIANT 1993. SANTA BARBARA. POT-SHOTS NO. 6204.

A
VIGOROUS
OLD AGE

USUALLY
STARTS
WITH
A VIGOROUS
YOUNG AGE.

Ashleigh Brilliant

© ASHLEIGH BRILLIANT 1992. SANTA BARBARA. POT-SHOTS NO. 6097.

I'M ALREADY TIRED
FROM MY
JOURNEY~

AND
IT HASN'T
EVEN
BEGUN YET!

Ashleigh Brilliant

© ASHLEIGH BRILLIANT 1995. SANTA BARBARA. POT-SHOTS NO. 6824.

NOBODY IS EVER COMPLETELY UNEMPLOYED ~ WE ALL HAVE A JOB CALLED GETTING THROUGH LIFE.

Ashleigh Brilliant

© ASHLEIGH BRILLIANT 1998. SANTA BARBARA. POT-SHOTS NO. 7865.

THIS FOOD IS GUARANTEED TO HAVE TOO MANY CALORIES.

Ashleigh Brilliant

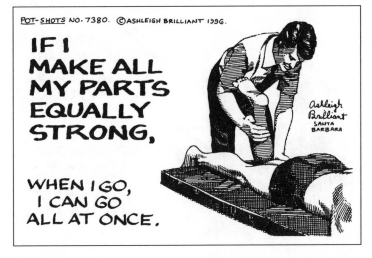

POT-SHOTS NO. 7380. © ASHLEIGH BRILLIANT 1996.

IF I MAKE ALL MY PARTS EQUALLY STRONG, WHEN I GO, I CAN GO ALL AT ONCE.

Ashleigh Brilliant SANTA BARBARA

© ASHLEIGH BRILLIANT 1995. POT-SHOTS NO. 6921.

NO ONE EVER TAUGHT ME HOW TO DREAM ~

IT'S JUST A NATURAL TALENT.

Ashleigh Brilliant
SANTA BARBARA

© ASHLEIGH BRILLIANT 1998. SANTA BARBARA. POT-SHOTS NO. 7885.

THE PERSON WHO COMES BACK

IS NEVER QUITE THE SAME AS THE ONE WHO WENT AWAY.

Ashleigh Brilliant

© ASHLEIGH BRILLIANT 1990. POT-SHOTS NO. 5150.

IT'S ALL RIGHT TO HAVE FUN WHILE WORKING,

SO LONG AS THE WORK DOESN'T INTERFERE WITH THE FUN.

Ashleigh Brilliant
SANTA BARBARA

© ASHLEIGH BRILLIANT 1993. SANTA BARBARA.

POT-SHOTS NO. 6324.

Ashleigh Brilliant

THE PROBLEM REQUIRES MORE STUDY, BECAUSE OTHERWISE THOSE STUDYING IT WILL BE OUT OF WORK.

POT-SHOTS NO. 355

Ashleigh Brilliant

ANY FRIEND OF THE EARTH IS A FRIEND OF MINE.

© BRILLIANT ENTERPRISES 1972

CHINESE: 天下爲公

POT-SHOTS NO. 6926

© ASHLEIGH BRILLIANT 1995. SANTA BARBARA.

EVERYBODY WANTS TO TRAVEL BY THE SHORTEST POSSIBLE ROUTE, SO WE'LL HAVE TO PAVE EVERYTHING.

Ashleigh Brilliant

Diverse Devotions   135

© ASHLEIGH BRILLIANT 1993. SANTA BARBARA.   POT-SHOTS NO. 6415.

THE ACTIVE INGREDIENT

IN MANY VERY EFFECTIVE HOME REMEDIES

IS CALLED FAITH.

Ashleigh Brilliant

© ASHLEIGH BRILLIANT 1995. SANTA BARBARA.   POT-SHOTS NO. 6941.

NO TWO PLACES HAVE EXACTLY THE SAME VIEW ~

THAT'S WHY TRAVEL EXPANDS YOUR VISION.

Ashleigh Brilliant

© ASHLEIGH BRILLIANT 1990.   POT-SHOTS NO. 5228.

YOU CAN'T SAY I'VE DONE NOTHING TODAY ~

YOU CAN ONLY SAY I'VE DONE NOTHING WORTHWHILE.

Ashleigh Brilliant
SANTA BARBARA

© ASHLEIGH BRILLIANT 1995.   POT-SHOTS NO. 6796.

**MY FEET
CAN TRAVEL
IN ANY
DIRECTION,**

BUT
MY HEART
ALWAYS POINTS HOME.

Ashleigh Brilliant
SANTA BARBARA

© ASHLEIGH BRILLIANT 1996.
SANTA
BARBARA   POT-SHOTS NO. 7051.

How are children
able to see
so much
that isn't there,

and overlook
so much
that is?

Ashleigh Brilliant

© ASHLEIGH BRILLIANT 1991.   POT-SHOTS NO. 5437.

**ONE VERY EFFECTIVE
FORM OF
RECREATIONAL
ACTIVITY**

IS
KNOWN AS
HARD
WORK.

Ashleigh Brilliant
SANTA BARBARA

© ASHLEIGH BRILLIANT 1995.   POT-SHOTS NO. 6734.

SOMETIMES
I FEEL THE NEED
TO CLEAN OUT
MY ENTIRE SYSTEM
WITH A GOOD DOSE
OF COOKIES.

Ashleigh Brilliant
SANTA BARBARA

© ASHLEIGH BRILLIANT 1996. SANTA BARBARA.   POT-SHOTS NO. 7275.

HERE'S THE WAY
TO LIVE
AND DIE:

KEEP GOING
AS LONG
AS YOU CAN ~

AND THEN STOP.

Ashleigh Brilliant

© ASHLEIGH BRILLIANT 1991.   POT-SHOTS NO. 5475.

WHAT CAN
I DO? ~

FOOD
MAKES ME
HAPPY,
AND HAPPINESS
MAKES ME
HUNGRY.

Ashleigh Brilliant
SANTA BARBARA

Diverse Devotions   139

© ASHLEIGH BRILLIANT 1995. POT-SHOTS NO. 6877.

OLD PEOPLE CAN REMEMBER BEING YOUNG,

BUT
YOUNG PEOPLE
CAN'T EVEN
IMAGINE
BEING OLD.

Ashleigh Brilliant
SANTA BARBARA

© ASHLEIGH BRILLIANT 1998. POT-SHOTS NO. 7739.

THE MORE
YOU KNOW
ABOUT
WHERE
YOU'RE
GOING,

THE LESS
YOUR
JOURNEY
IS AN
ADVENTURE.

Ashleigh Brilliant
SANTA BARBARA

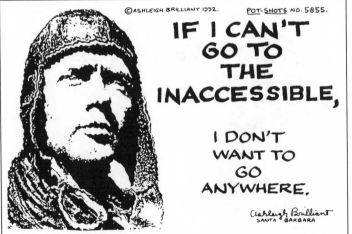

© ASHLEIGH BRILLIANT 1992. POT-SHOTS NO. 5855.

IF I CAN'T GO TO THE INACCESSIBLE,

I DON'T
WANT TO
GO
ANYWHERE.

Ashleigh Brilliant
SANTA BARBARA

140

© ASHLEIGH BRILLIANT 1998 · SANTA BARBARA.   POT-SHOTS NO. 7765.

EVERYONE KNOWS WHO FIRST WALKED ON THE MOON,

BUT NOBODY KNOWS WHO FIRST WALKED ON THE EARTH.

Ashleigh Brilliant

© ASHLEIGH BRILLIANT 1995. SANTA BARBARA   POT-SHOTS NO. 6881.

LIFE IS TOO SHORT

TO BE FRITTERED AWAY ON EFFORTS TO LENGTHEN IT.

Ashleigh Brilliant

© ASHLEIGH BRILLIANT 1996 · SANTA BARBARA.   POT-SHOTS NO. 7508.

I don't see how Heaven can possibly be any better than Earth at its best.

Ashleigh Brilliant

Diverse Devotions   141

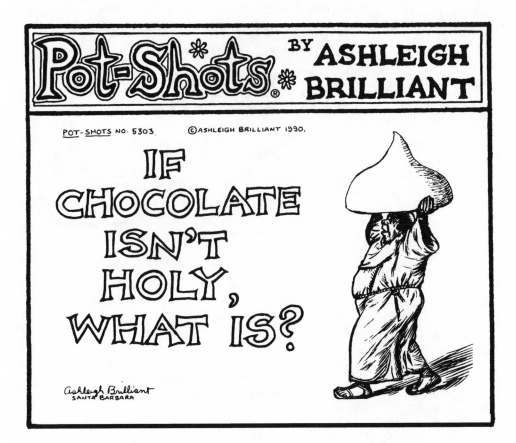

XI. Out of My Mind

What have we here? If Thought itself is in some ways an article of Faith, then the myriad MISCELLANEOUS MUSINGS which meander through my mind must surely deserve a Chapter of their own in this volume.

I have been thinking from an early age. The first thought I can clearly remember having was based on direct observation: It was that there were people in the world taller than my father. This was unsettling—and my thoughts have remained unsettled ever since (as you have probably already gathered).

I myself, who am of average height, actually grew to be taller than my father. But I must somehow have assumed as an infant that my parents were the pattern of all humankind. (In this delusion I was hardly alone. Much later in life, I read that a young son of Charles Darwin, whose unusual home was full of biological experiments and specimens, was said to have asked, upon first visiting a playmate's house, "Where does your father do his barnacles?")

The whole thinking process seems to be one of determining that our previous thoughts were wrong— of replacing old patterns with new ones. This is hard enough for even an amateur thinker, but the task has been made even more challenging in my professional case by having to think every new thought in 17 words or less. Brevity is not a characteristic of most inspired writing, even though the authors of sacred texts are not generally paid by the word. The secret is, of course, to eliminate everything not absolutely essential. Unfortunately, that secret won't get you very far, since, as any truly enlightened thinker knows, nothing in this world is really essential.

©ASHLEIGH BRILLIANT 1996. SANTA BARBARA

POT-SHOTS NO. 7035.

WHAT MATTERS IS NOT WHETHER THE REMEDY IS BASED ON SCIENCE OR FAITH,

BUT WHETHER IT WORKS.

Ashleigh Brilliant

©ASHLEIGH BRILLIANT 1993. SANTA BARBARA.

POT-SHOTS NO. 6223.

THE MOST IMPORTANT OF ALL COLOR DIFFERENCES

IS THAT BETWEEN A RED LIGHT AND A GREEN LIGHT.

Ashleigh Brilliant

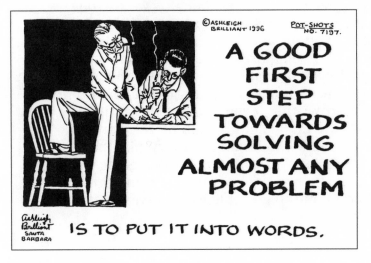

©ASHLEIGH BRILLIANT 1996

POT-SHOTS NO. 7197.

A GOOD FIRST STEP TOWARDS SOLVING ALMOST ANY PROBLEM

Ashleigh Brilliant
SANTA BARBARA

IS TO PUT IT INTO WORDS.

144

© ASHLEIGH BRILLIANT 1996. SANTA BARBARA.   POT-SHOTS NO. 7335.

IN THE INTERNATIONAL
CHEATING COMPETITION,

I SCORED ELEVEN
OUT OF A POSSIBLE TEN.

Ashleigh Brilliant

© ASHLEIGH BRILLIANT 1998. SANTA BARBARA.   POT-SHOTS NO. 8000.

Ashleigh Brilliant

I'VE SEEN
SO MANY
THINGS
I NEVER
EXPECTED
TO SEE

THAT NOW
I EXPECT
TO SEE EVERYTHING.

© ASHLEIGH BRILLIANT 1983.   POT-SHOTS NO. 2859.

ANIMALS
HAVE WONDERFUL WAYS
OF PROTECTING THEMSELVES

AGAINST
ALMOST
EVERYTHING,

EXCEPT
US.

Ashleigh Brilliant

146

© ASHLEIGH BRILLIANT 1995
SANTA BARBARA

POT-SHOTS NO. 6714.
Ashleigh Brilliant

DO COINCIDENCES HAVE MEANING?

IF SO, THEY'RE NOT JUST COINCIDENCES.

© ASHLEIGH BRILLIANT 1998.

POT-SHOTS NO. 7594.

I'M NOT READY FOR THE FUTURE,

AND SEEM TO BE GETTING LESS READY ALL THE TIME.

Ashleigh Brilliant
SANTA BARBARA

© ASHLEIGH BRILLIANT 1995. SANTA BARBARA.

POT-SHOTS NO. 6721.

ALMOST EVERYBODY WOULD LIKE TO CHANGE SOMEBODY'S MIND —

BUT VERY FEW MINDS ACTUALLY WANT TO BE CHANGED.

Ashleigh Brilliant

© ASHLEIGH BRILLIANT 1998.   POT-SHOTS NO. 7712.

PROMISE ME YOU'LL NEVER MARRY ME!

Ashleigh Brilliant
SANTA BARBARA

© ASHLEIGH BRILLIANT 1991.   POT-SHOTS NO. 5465.

IF I COULD ALWAYS THINK PERFECTLY CLEARLY,

I COULD NEVER SLEEP, OR FALL IN LOVE.

Ashleigh Brilliant
SANTA BARBARA

© ASHLEIGH BRILLIANT 1995. SANTA BARBARA.   POT-SHOTS NO. 6876.

THIS PLACE IS FULL

OF ABSENT FRIENDS.

Ashleigh Brilliant

© ASHLEIGH BRILLIANT 1998. POT-SHOTS NO. 7802.

IF ONLY GREAT COOKING
COULD BE RECORDED,
LIKE OTHER GREAT PERFORMANCES,

AND EATEN OVER AND OVER AGAIN!

© ASHLEIGH BRILLIANT 1992. POT-SHOTS NO. 5927.

SOMETIMES IT REQUIRES
A VERY CLEAR DAY
IN ORDER TO SEE
THE OBVIOUS.

© ASHLEIGH BRILLIANT 1996. SANTA BARBARA. POT-SHOTS NO. 7098.

ANIMALS CAN BE TAUGHT
TO BEHAVE LIKE PEOPLE,

AND PEOPLE ALREADY KNOW HOW TO BEHAVE LIKE ANIMALS.

© ASHLEIGH BRILLIANT 1998. SANTA BARBARA. POT-SHOTS NO. 7870.

SELF-PRESERVATION IS THE FIRST LAW OF NATURE,

BUT IT'S NOT ALWAYS CONSIDERED GOOD MANNERS.

Ashleigh Brilliant

© ASHLEIGH BRILLIANT 1993. SANTA BARBARA. POT-SHOTS NO. 6141.

THE DIFFERENCE BETWEEN THE GUEST AND THE HOST

IS THAT ONLY THE GUEST CAN GO HOME.

Ashleigh Brilliant

© ASHLEIGH BRILLIANT 1996. SANTA BARBARA POT-SHOTS NO. 7114.

If you know A causes B,

and you really don't want B,

my advice is: avoid A.

Ashleigh Brilliant

© ASHLEIGH BRILLIANT 1998. SANTA BARBARA.

POT-SHOTS NO. 7944.

THERE'S NO SUCH THING AS THE RIGHT TO BE COMFORTABLE

— BUT THERE OUGHT TO BE!

Ashleigh Brilliant

© ASHLEIGH BRILLIANT 1995.

POT-SHOTS NO. 6943.

THERE ARE SOME EXCELLENT BOOKS ON HOW TO SAVE TIME ~

~ BUT I HAVEN'T TIME TO READ THEM.

Ashleigh Brilliant
SANTA BARBARA

© ASHLEIGH BRILLIANT 1998. SANTA BARBARA.

POT-SHOTS NO. 8119.

IN MY IDEAL WORLD,

WE'D ALL GO DIRECTLY FROM CHILDHOOD TO RETIREMENT.

Ashleigh Brilliant

XII. Soothe Sayings

Relax! There's nothing threatening here. After so arduous a passage through eleven challenging chapters of dither and doubt, this final stage of your pilgrimage seeks to calm and strengthen you with thoughts of INSPIRATION and CONSOLATION. Where did they come from? There must be some secret spring of hope and joy trickling out of the dark recesses of my benighted soul.

We are not, of course, at the end of the road—this is just another way-station on life's journey. But if coming even this far has to any degree been difficult for you, think how much harder it has been for me! And remember that *you* can always walk away from this book, and forget all about it—while I, for better or worse, am locked here in it forever.

But we both know, if we have any Faith at all, that we're bound to meet again some day on a Farther Shore, in some celestial Happy Hunting Ground (equally happy, one must hope, both for the hunters and for the hunted). In the meantime, the important thing is not to lose what Faith we have. (You may have noticed, however, that those who do lose Faith rarely advertise for its return—a fact which may in itself offer a measure of solace.)

So prepare the cockles of your heart to be warmed, here in the Comfort Zone of Brilliant Thoughts. Although I probably can't provide you with total Salvation, you may at least experience a few modest Revelations. And keep in mind that if, in the end, the mountain still refuses to budge, you can always go back to moving clouds.

© ASHLEIGH BRILLIANT 1993. SANTA BARBARA.

POT-SHOTS NO. 6161

THINGS DON'T ALWAYS GO AS HOPED OR PLANNED ~

BUT THAT'S NO REASON TO STOP HOPING AND PLANNING.

Ashleigh Brilliant

© ASHLEIGH BRILLIANT 1996. SANTA BARBARA.

POT-SHOTS NO. 7399.

IF YOU CAN'T LOSE YOUR SADNESS,

TRY TO TURN IT INTO SOMETHING BEAUTIFUL.

Ashleigh Brilliant

© ASHLEIGH BRILLIANT 1998. SANTA BARBARA.

POT-SHOTS NO. 8066.

ONE WAY TO INCREASE THE AMOUNT OF KINDNESS IN THE WORLD

is by being kinder to yourself.

Ashleigh Brilliant

NOT EVERYONE WHO STARTS CAN WIN,

BUT IT'S EVEN HARDER TO WIN, IF YOU NEVER START.

POT-SHOTS NO. 2021.

© ASHLEIGH BRILLIANT 1980

Ashleigh Brilliant

© ASHLEIGH BRILLIANT 1993. SANTA BARBARA.

POT-SHOTS NO. 6238.

Ashleigh Brilliant

IF YOU MUST WASTE YOUR LIFE,

TRY TO DO IT IN A CREATIVE AND ORIGINAL WAY.

© ASHLEIGH BRILLIANT 1996. SANTA BARBARA.

POT-SHOTS NO. 7405.

Ashleigh Brilliant

THE STRONGEST ALWAYS WINS IN THE END ~

BUT DON'T FORGET THAT THERE ARE DIFFERENT KINDS OF STRENGTH.

© ASHLEIGH BRILLIANT 1982

Ashleigh Brilliant

POT-SHOTS NO. 2409.

If you postpone a pleasure long enough, it may melt, spoil, die, evaporate, or move away.

© ASHLEIGH BRILLIANT 1993.
SANTA BARBARA

Ashleigh Brilliant

POT-SHOTS NO. 6261.

STOP WORRYING! WITH JUST ONE SMALL EXCEPTION, NO SINGLE DAY OF YOUR LIFE WILL BE THE LAST.

© ASHLEIGH BRILLIANT 1996 SANTA BARBARA

POT-SHOTS NO. 7472

WE DON'T COME FROM NOTHING AND RETURN TO NOTHING ~ we come from everything, and return to everything.

Ashleigh Brilliant

160

©ASHLEIGH BRILLIANT 1993. SANTA BARBARA

POT-SHOTS NO. 6276.

Life may be the price we have to pay for all that lovely time in eternity.

Ashleigh Brilliant

©ASHLEIGH BRILLIANT 1998.

POT-SHOTS NO. 7564.

COMFORTING THOUGHT:

FAR MORE PEOPLE IN THE WORLD MEAN TO DO GOOD THAN MEAN TO DO BAD.

Ashleigh Brilliant
SANTA BARBARA

©ASHLEIGH BRILLIANT 1990.

POT-SHOTS NO. 5217.

If you can't overcome your temptations, try to overcome your sense of guilt.

Ashleigh Brilliant
SANTA BARBARA

Soothe Sayings 161

© ASHLEIGH BRILLIANT 1993. SANTA BARBARA.

POT-SHOTS NO. 6322.

WHAT MATTERS IS NOT THAT YOU KEEP FALLING OFF,

BUT THAT YOU KEEP GETTING BACK ON.

© ASHLEIGH BRILLIANT 1998. SANTA BARBARA.

POT-SHOTS NO. 7631.

LIFE MUST BE A GOOD THING ~

WHY ELSE WOULD PEOPLE BE SO EAGER TO PASS IT ON?

© ASHLEIGH BRILLIANT 1991

POT-SHOTS NO. 5329.

THE WORLD IS NOT YET PERFECT ~

THAT'S THE BEST REASON FOR STAYING ALIVE.

© ASHLEIGH BRILLIANT 1995. SANTA BARBARA.

POT-SHOTS NO. 6653.

Ashleigh Brilliant

THE BEST THING ABOUT BEING LOST AND FORGOTTEN IS THE JOY OF BEING RE-DISCOVERED.

© ASHLEIGH BRILLIANT 1998. SANTA BARBARA.

POT-SHOTS NO. 7746.

Ashleigh Brilliant

THE DIFFERENCE BETWEEN ACCEPTANCE AND REJECTION IS THAT WHEN YOU'RE ACCEPTED, YOU DON'T HAVE TO TRY AGAIN.

© ASHLEIGH BRILLIANT 1991.

POT-SHOTS NO. 5395.

TRY TO BE HAPPY, TRY TO BE GOOD,

AND TRY NOT TO SEE THIS AS A CONTRADICTION.

Ashleigh Brilliant
SANTA BARBARA

Soothe Sayings 163

© ASHLEIGH BRILLIANT 1995. SANTA BARBARA.

POT-SHOTS NO. 6810

THE POWER TO PUNISH

IS NOT
AS GREAT
AS
THE POWER
TO FORGIVE.

© ASHLEIGH BRILLIANT 1998. SANTA BARBARA

POT-SHOTS NO. 7792.

TRY TO TAKE PRIDE IN SOMETHING ~

WHETHER IT'S
YOUR NOBEL PRIZE

OR JUST THAT
YOU'RE SOBER TODAY.

Ashleigh Brilliant

© ASHLEIGH BRILLIANT 1992.

POT-SHOTS NO. 5801.

CALAMITIES COME IN ALL SHAPES AND SIZES,

BUT
SO DO
OPPORTUNITIES.

Ashleigh Brilliant
SANTA BARBARA

Appendix: Brilliant versus Brinkley

(See Title Waive, *Page 15.)*

David Brinkley
111 East Melrose Street
Chevy Chase, Maryland 20815

March 7, 1997

Mr. ASHLEIGH BRILLIANT
Brilliant Enterprises
117 West Valerio Street
Santa Barbara,
California 93101

Dear Mr. Brilliant:

Thank you for your letter.

In reference to the <u>Wall Street Journal</u> story and your objection to its terminology, I do not remember now whether I did or did not use the word "shakedown," but in any case I hold no such opinion of my dealings with you, and further I am told that in several court rulings the word has been held to be mere slang.

Again, I offer above my feeling about our dealings and my best wishes to you.

Sincerely,

David Brinkley

Making Ends Meet

The end of something is always the beginning of something else. (Isn't that ultimately what Faith is all about?) I hope you've enjoyed rubbing your mind up against mine, here in this strange meeting place we call a book. If you have, let's keep in touch.

There is now an exciting new way we can get together. Like many other mortals, I have dragged myself kicking and screaming into the age of electronic communication. I maintain what is currently called a Website, where you can (at least theoretically) reach me instantaneously at any time from anywhere in the world. The address is:

http://www.AshleighBrilliant.com

Brilliant Thoughts exist and circulate in many other forms, including postcards, a variety of licensed products, and a syndicated newspaper feature. If by chance you have your own special use in mind for any of my material, my Permissions Department will be very happy to hear from you.

Whatever your interest, allow me to recommend that you first send for my Catalogue, which is your key to a whole handy, helpful, hysterical world of Brilliant messages. The current (1998) price is just two U.S. dollars. Please enclose that amount, or its equivalent in your own time and currency.

Yours most faithfully,

Ashleigh Brilliant
117 W. Valerio Street,
Santa Barbara, California 93101, U.S.A.
WWW.ASHLEIGHBRILLIANT.COM